"Doing Justice" in the People's Court

SUNY Series, "New Directions in Crime and Justice Studies"
Austin T. Turk, Editor

"Doing Justice" in the People's Court

Sentencing by Municipal Court Judges

Jon'a Meyer
and
Paul Jesilow

State University of New York Press

Published by
State University of New York Press, Albany

© 1997 State University of New York

For information, address State University of New York
Press, State University Plaza, Albany, N.Y., 12246

Production by E. Moore
Marketing by Bernadette LaManna

Library of Congress Cataloging-in-Publication Data

Meyer, Jon'a, 1967-
    "Doing Justice" in the people's court : sentencing by municipal
court judges / Jon'a Meyer, Paul Jesilow.
        p.   cm. — (SUNY series in new directions in crime and justice
studies)
    Includes bibliographical references and index.
    ISBN 0-7914-3137-1 (alk. paper). — ISBN 0-7914-3138-X (pbk. :
alk. paper)
    1. Municipal courts—United States. 2. Sentences (Criminal
procedure)—United States. 3. Judicial process—United States.
    4. Discrimination in criminal justice administration—United States.
I. Jesilow, Paul, 1950-   . II. Title. III. Series.
KF8737.M49   1997
347.73'22—dc20
[347.3072]   96—3774
                                                                          CIP

10   9   8   7   6   5   4   3   2   1

For our parents, Jon and Faye, Rosalie and Ted,
who raised us well—and for Gil Geis,
who taught us more than academic lessons.

Malama pono, Malama i na kupuna.

Be righteous and cherish the heritage of our ancestors.

CONTENTS

PREFACE

Although some in society likely believe judicial careers await only those embodying divine qualities (e.g., wisdom and patience), judges are usually far less hallowed. Routinely drawn from local communities, magistrates tend to represent the values of those with whom they share their neighborhoods. Judges are, after all, human and their perceptions of justice may be more likely related to their personal characteristics than their immeasurable wisdom. The fear, of course, is that the punishments they dispense will reflect the justices' individual biases and that sentences will not be equitable. Since each judge weights the various factors differently, inconsistent sentences will result.

Concern with judicial imposition of criminal penalties is by no means a new phenomenon. Cesare Beccaria (1775/1983) based much of his call for legislative determination of laws and punishments on his belief that differences between judges led to disparate uses of sanctions. Indeed, many studies have been conducted to uncover hypothesized prejudices attributed to race/ethnicity, socioeconomic status, gender, age, and a host of other extralegal factors that may become known or conjectured by judges during court hearings.

Recent sentencing guidelines at the felony level have severely limited judicial discretion, but in the state municipal courts, where the bulk of criminal cases are adjudicated, judges are free to fashion penalties based on individual ideology. Sentences resulting from the differing doctrines may lead to feelings of oppression by those who receive the more severe punishments. Evidence of judicial bias in sentencing also hurts the image of equality in our democratic society; disturbances in the delicate balance of trust vested in our criminal justice system may have dire outcomes; for example (although not the result of judicial action), the urban rebellion in Los Angeles following the acquittal of officers who were videotaped beating Rodney King, a crime suspect.

There are many critics of the court system. The police, for one, feel that judges are too lenient. The minorities and poor in society, however, fear that justices give them the heavy-handed portion of punishments. They believe that favoritism is granted to the white middle and upper class and that the jails are filled with those from less advantageous circumstances.

Defenders of the criminal justice system posit that the inequitable distribution of the poor in jails and prisons is due to repeated crimes on their part. Critics of the system agree that having a prior criminal record is more likely to land one in jail, but retort that because of bias the poor are disproportionately more likely to be stopped, arrested, and found guilty of crimes. At the felony level, prior record is a major determinate of eventual punishments, but prior records are usually established in the lower courts. The concern is that misdemeanor judges may cause systemic inequities by punishing offenders based on the color of their skin or the size of their bank accounts.

This manuscript combines information gathered from interviews with municipal court judges and data collected from observations of misdemeanor arraignments in their courtrooms to shed light on what factors the judges used in making sentencing decisions. Chapter 1 discusses the operation and issues associated with the municipal courts. It notes that sentencing is affected by more than judges' individual ideologies. The need for judges, prosecutors, and defense attorneys to efficiently process thousands of cases proves a major influence on the punishments defendants receive.

Chapter 2 reviews the literature on sentencing in criminal courts and the judicial biases that may affect court decisions. A great deal of research has been conducted to determine whether and under what circumstances extralegal factors, such as race and gender, affect severity of criminal sentences. Most of these studies, however, have depended more on increasing sophistication in research methodologies and/or statistical techniques than well-formed research plans. Although academic research necessarily involves building upon earlier works and increasing sophistication as improved methods become available, the research on judicial bias in sentencing can best be described as a methodological battle that intensified with each new publication. Researchers appear to react to the work of others in the field by submitting a study that is "superior," due to more sophisticated methods or better choice of variables. The methodological quagmire is examined in some detail in this chapter.

Chapter 3 presents the results of interviews with the lower court judges and discusses their ideas about sentencing. Judges we interviewed perceived their function in the courts as "doing justice" and judicial discretion, they posited, was essential if they were to discharge this job. As a result, they endeavored to expand their use of mechanisms that gave them greater options. The judges' stated attempts to "do justice," however, also suggested a way in which inequities may creep into judicial decisions, as their formulations often included extralegal factors, such as defendants' attitudes or motivations for committing their offenses. Bias, as reflected in our interviews with judges, does not involve active decisions against members of certain groups. Rather, it is more subtle and introduced by judicial attitudes that favor middle class values.

Chapter 4 portrays the work of the courts and examines the factors that lead criminal defendants to plead guilty. The data on which we base our observations were derived from 1,600 misdemeanor arraignment hearings collected by trained observers in the courtrooms of justices we had interviewed. A total of 135 separate offenses were identified ranging from commonly known offenses such as driving under the influence of alcohol and petty theft to less well known offenses such as going through refuse and fueling a boat while docking.

Chapter 5 further examines a subset of those who were arraigned. We focused on the sentences handed out to defendants who pled guilty to examine factors that are important in the municipal court judges' decision making. We did not intend to prove or disprove the existence of judicial bias. We begin with the assumption that bias exists. Obviously, from what the judges told us, similar offenders may be sentenced differentially—some may be treated leniently, while others receive the full measure of the law. The purpose of our analyses was to illuminate the complex conditions under which bias may occur and the factors that give rise to it.

The question is not whether bias exists, but rather what kinds of biases exist, under what circumstances are they maximized, and under what situations are they minimized.

Finally, chapter 6 discusses our findings and conclusions with respect to these matters and provides suggestions for change.

ACKNOWLEDGMENTS

We owe special thanks to the many research assistants and others who helped us at all stages of the research project. The project may not have taken place without the assistance of Helen Ahn, Yohannes Assefa, Eugene Cruz, Darren Field, Mary Lou Franco, Carrie Huntington, Sophie Kim, Jean Langevin, Claudia Lavenant, Christine Le, Allison Lee, Michael Leventhal, Ron Milkes, Constance O'Connor, Tracy Olgin, Silvia San Martin, Younosha Thomas, and Alyssa Weisbach.

We would also like to thank Gilbert Geis, James Meeker, and Joan Petersilia for their comments on earlier versions. A special debt is owed to Judy Omiya, who put up with our constant requests with continuing good nature.

We also wish to thank the judges and courtroom staff who participated in this study. To ensure the anonymity we promised them, their names go unmentioned. We greatly appreciate the time and effort they gave the project and their participation shows that those in the system have a true desire to make sure that justice is evenly distributed.

Lastly, we thank our friends and family, who have been tremendous sources of happiness and support for us when times were difficult. We thank them all, but foremost among them are Gloria and Tom Bogdan, Judy Case, Diana Grant, Tara Gray, Carolyn Kuali`i, and Deborah Parsons (and Zackary).

Some financial support was provided by the American Sociological Association Dissertation Support Funds, the National Institutes of Mental Health, and the National Science Foundation Minority Fellowship Program for which we are thankful.

CHAPTER 1

MUNICIPAL COURTS AND THE JUDGES WHO SIT IN THEM

The judge's gavel pounds furiously as though it has a life of its own, while cries of "Order in the court!" fall on seemingly deaf ears. The courtroom observers appear out of control, leaping up and yelling, some rushing toward the door while others charge to the front of the room. There are gasps of disbelief from all in the court, including the surprised prosecutor. Yet another witness for the prosecution has wavered under the crafty questioning of Perry Mason and confessed to murder, saving an innocent woman from, at best, life in prison.

In another courtroom, the prosecutor and defense attorney battle to the finish, jumping up with expertly timed objections to every question asked by opposing counsel. After intense consideration of each objection, the judge issues a ruling and the attorney rewords the question to the witness, an elderly woman on whose eyewitness testimony the prosecution's entire murder cases rests. When court is recessed until the next day, the two attorneys briskly walk by one another, hardly exchanging even a cold glance. Everyone in the room knows the two will be back at each other's throats when court resumes on the following day, like the ferocious adversaries opposing counsel are supposed to be. During the trial, the media mill about outside the hearing like hungry hounds waiting for a morsel of news to fall from the courtroom table. Such is a day on "LA Law," a syndicated television series that focused on the activities of a Los Angeles–based law firm and its staff.

The public's picture of courtrooms and judges' activities have been largely shaped over the last forty years by television and movie depictions. Even real courtroom scenes on television are dramatic. The trial of the police officers who had beaten Rodney King, for example, earned prime-time coverage because of its great importance. Likewise, the preliminary hearing and trial of O.J. Simpson received a great deal of news coverage because the defendant was a celebrity. Even uninteresting incidents took on added significance when portrayed in Judge Wopner's courtroom on "The People's Court." For years, viewers tuned in daily to hear Wopner rule on cases in which he decided, for example, who would have to pay for the broken rearview mirror on the plaintiff's Honda.

The courtroom depictions portrayed on television and in the movies are understood by the lay public to represent the inner workings of the criminal judiciary. Justice is always served in these courts. Defense attorneys, like Perry Mason or Ben Matlock, always battle to the finish for their innocent clients. Prosecutors are sneaky, less than honorable individuals who will stop at nothing to obtain convictions. If not for the valiant efforts of defense attorneys, innocent defendants would be executed or sent to prison for crimes they did not commit.

Media judges are regal, emotionless creatures in flowing black robes who ponder each motion and objection, rendering a well-formed decision. Judges are more like baseball umpires than members of the courtroom group; they coordinate the activities of the prosecution and defense to ensure that both play by fair rules, but media judges refuse to become involved in the courtroom happenings and rarely get personally absorbed in a case.

The lone exception to media courtrooms, "Night Court," does not focus on the cases processed each day; instead, it centers on the staff of the court and their interactions, which often have little to do with handling cases. Even the bailiff and court clerk have major roles in the show. The sleazeball prosecutor is always up to no good; if he is not picking up on every woman in the courthouse, he is losing large sums of money on nefarious ventures. The defense attorney, a feminist, yet feminine, woman would never willingly socialize with the likes of the prosecutor and often feels uncomfortable when he is in the same room. The judge is an amateur magician who frequently demonstrates his magic tricks to the defendants whose cases are being heard; he is a friendly and compassionate fellow who leads the viewer to wonder why he is trapped in the doldrums of municipal court, doomed forever to hear prostitution cases. The reality of the criminal courts is far from these colorful portraits, which are based more on the American dream of justice than fact. High drama is rarely the stuff of real courts. Courtroom happenings are seldom as exciting as shows like "LA Law" would have their audiences believe. Defense attorneys almost never get a witness to confess on the stand like Perry Mason or Ben Matlock do in nearly every episode. The workings of the courts tend to be uninteresting to the observer, full of whispered sidebar conferences between the judge and attorneys, meetings behind the scenes in the judge's chambers, and legal motions that are difficult for the layperson to understand.

Murder, armed robbery, and rape cases are routinely tried before juries on television, but in the real world, less than 5 percent of all felony filings result in criminal trials (Boland, Mahanna, & Sones, 1992). In fact, courtroom dramas do not depict the reality of courts because almost all of America's criminal cases are processed in municipal courtrooms.

MUNICIPAL COURTS

Unlike federal and felony-level magistrates, municipal judges and their courtrooms have been the subjects of very little research and are the least understood branch of the judiciary (to ease the reader's burden, we use the terms judge, justice, and magistrate interchangeably). One court expert commented: "Many individuals get into and out of trouble in these [urban] courts, but the general public knows almost nothing about their operation" (Jacob, 1980, p. 93). Researchers, too, know little about municipal court judges; the academic literature has virtually ignored them (Alfini & Passuth, 1981;

Brickey & Miller, 1975; Feeley, 1979, p. xvi). They are very important, however, because the lower court judges handle most of the judiciary's criminal work load and their actions serve as a focal point for the formation of public opinion about the entire court system (Brickey & Miller, 1975).

Ninety percent of criminal cases in the United States are heard in the municipal or other lower courts (Ashman, 1975; Feeley, 1979, p. xv). Generally, municipal judges hear misdemeanors, which are offenses that can be punished by less than one year in jail.[1] These tribunals also serve as the beginning point for felony cases (offenses that can be punished by any term of imprisonment or the death penalty), which can later be transferred to higher state courts.[2] They also serve as the "principle forum for negotiating the settlement of private disputes" by acting as neutral arbitrators between acquaintances in minor criminal offenses and petty civil claims cases (Ashman, 1975, p. 3).

The municipal courts are busy. In California, nearly 9,000,000 cases (not counting parking offenses) were disposed of by municipal court judges during the 1990–91 fiscal year, for an average of more than 11,000 cases per judicial position (Judicial Council of California, 1992, p. 78), or an average of 43 cases per day per judge. In contrast, California's superior courts (which process felony cases) disposed of 825,935 cases the same year, for an average of 865 per judicial position or 3 a day (Judicial Council of California, 1992, p. 41). If only in terms of sheer volume, municipal court is truly where the action is.

When the public has contact with the judiciary, it is most likely with municipal judges. A courtroom researcher observed that one municipal court judge in Texas saw over 100,000 people (including defendants, witnesses, jurors, and friends of the various participants) during the course of one year, and "all were forming their impressions of our system of laws in that judge's court" (Ashman, 1975, p. 588).

Although they may enter with idealized visions of what happens in court from dramatic portrayals in the media, it is in the lower tribunals that defendants, complainants, witnesses, jurors, and bystanders form their opinions of the criminal justice system (Brickey & Miller, 1975) and "often they come away with a less-than-favorable impression" (Neubauer, 1984, p. 358).

BRIEF HISTORY OF MUNICIPAL COURT JUDGES

The manner in which municipal court judges dispose of their cases is rooted in the history of the lower courts. Misdemeanor crimes came into existence in the 1700s. Few legal offenses existed at the time and those that did had severe punishments attached to them, death or loss of property being the most common ones. The creation in England of misdemeanors, or lesser crimes to be punished by a fine, allowed the Crown to extend its control and provided it with a way to raise money (Lindquist, 1988, p. 15).

The introduction of municipal courts to the youthful United States was a response to the democratic, rural nature of its inhabitants. Modes of transportation available during the nation's infancy and the considerable distances between existing courts necessitated the birth of a local form of justice for those charged with the statutorily less serious misdemeanors. It did not make sense to transport many miles to a district court a person accused of a crime for which the maximum sentence was a short jail term or small fine. It was also perceived as inappropriate to make an accused person wait weeks to be tried. The municipal courts were created to provide access to justice that was "responsive to early American needs" (Ashman, 1975, p. 4).

Depending on population size, a municipal court judge (for urban areas) or justice of the peace (for less densely populated rural areas) heard misdemeanor cases, settled local disputes, and occasionally added a local flair to justice. Although capable of providing some sort of equity, it seems likely that judicial decisions in these far flung tribunals were based more on local custom or personal gain and less on rule of law or systematic justice. Judges' rulings were often designed to ensure that some funds flowed their way. In one case, for example, the justice demanded that the victim's recovered property be sold to pay the fine he had just levied against the indigent thief. Vehement protests from the victim and his attorney only resulted in further loss of money as the judge was quick to fine them for their outbursts (*In Re Jesus Ramirez*, Tuolumne County, Case No. 516, printed in McClay & Matthews, 1991, p. 133).

For most of the nineteenth century the lower courts were scenes of little activity. Few minor infractions had been enacted and city police departments, which produce most of the defendants for today's municipal judiciary, did not exist. There was no need for full-time judges or permanent structures. They worked with little or no support staff. Few of the judges were educated in the law. They held their hearings in dilapidated buildings or makeshift courtrooms, stores and private homes.

In the late 1800s, increases in city populations, largely fueled by newly arrived immigrants, resulted in escalating crime. The addition of municipal police departments increased urban court caseloads to the extent that they overloaded the existing judicial system (Ashman, 1975, p. 5). Many scholars and courtroom observers felt that without increased support the municipal courts would soon crumble beneath their awesome caseloads and recommended that they be eliminated or subsumed by the felony court system (Geis, 1979; President's Commission Task Force Report on the Courts, 1967).

Assembly Lines Versus Justice

The municipal courts, of course, did not die, but neither did their excessive caseloads. If anything, the twentieth century has been accompanied by more work for the lower courts with many of today's judges handling more than 10,000 cases a year and some justices hearing in excess of 20,000 actions (The President's Commission Task Force Report on the Courts, 1967, p. 31; Ashman, 1975; Judicial Council of California 1992, pp. 78–81).

The concern with overloaded courts is that to accomplish their work judges, prosecutors, and defense counsel can spend no more than a minute with each case and justice is trampled in such circumstances (Lindquist, 1988, p. 24; Feeley, 1979, p. 11; Mileski, 1971). To speed arraignments, for example, defendants may be read their rights in groups or not at all (Mileski, 1971). The dilemma of huge caseloads versus due process of law, one expert noted, "is frequently resolved through bureaucratically ordained short cuts, deviations, and outright rule violations by members of the court, from judges to stenographers (Blumberg, 1967, p. xi)."

The most common way that members of the court deal with their excessive caseloads is by the use of plea bargains. These oft-repeated courtroom rituals involve negotiations between key players about the fates of defendants who plead guilty to criminal charges rather than exercising their rights to time consuming trials. Compliant defendants are typically rewarded with lesser punishments than they would receive if found guilty following a trial (Mileski, 1971).

Plea bargains in many courts are initiated by defense attorneys, who approach prosecutors with offers to "settle" cases. In a system that depends heavily on guilty pleas, this is one of the defense attorney's primary functions. Prosecutors may accept the offers of defense counsels or they may negotiate further (McCall, 1978, p. 99). In the end, the bargains are submitted to the presiding judges for approval, but the recommendations of the prosecutors and defense attorneys are usually followed (Cramer, 1981, p. 185; Feeley, 1979; Neubauer, 1976, p. 93).

ORGANIZATIONAL THEORY

The court system operates much as other organizations with a "community of human beings who are engaged in doing certain things with, to, and for each other" (Blumberg, 1967, p. ix). It is mutual cooperation between the key players in the court system that explains what happens in court, including sentencing decisions by judges.

Those who form the "courtroom work group" (the judge, prosecutor, and defense attorney) are driven by "incentives and shared goals" (Eisenstein and Jacob, 1977, p. 10). Further, these organizational goals may be more important when determining the severity of sentences handed out by judges than individual biases against any particular type of defendant (minorities, murderers, or recidivists, for example).

Judges, prosecutors, and defense attorneys have their own covert goals that coopt the ideals of justice (Blumberg, 1967; Eisenstein & Jacob, 1977; Mileski, 1971; Nardulli, 1978). Plea bargaining is the primary way these major players in the court system work together to achieve their individual goals (Blumberg, 1967; Eisenstein & Jacob, 1977; Nardulli, 1978).

Plea bargaining allows judges to "avoid the time consuming, expensive, unpredictable snares and pitfalls of an adversary trial" (Blumberg, 1967, p. 65). Trials require extra work for justices who have to familiarize themselves with prior legal reasoning in order to make educated decisions about motions submitted by defense and prosecuting attorneys. Judicial determinations also raise the possibility that appellate courts may at a later date disagree with the justices' reasoning and overturn their rulings: at best, a matter of embarrassment; at worst, expensive retrials and potential loss of their seats on the bench as dissatisfied electorates choose more efficient judges.

Judges are, to a certain extent, administrators. They must be able to handle excessive caseloads and shoulder their fair share of the judicial burden. Justices who are unable to guide satisfactory plea bargains will most likely be reproached by their brethren who have to pick up the courtroom slack.

Plea bargains also allow judges to "engage in a social-psychological fantasy" wherein the defendant has already admitted his guilt and stands before the judge as "an already repentant" individual (Blumberg, 1967, p. 65). Judges who value remorseful defendants may inflate the worth of this part of the plea bargaining ceremony, thus allowing themselves to feel better about leniently sentencing defendants who plead guilty.

Prosecutors also find plea bargaining advantageous. The government attorneys are evaluated on their ability to obtain convictions and plea bargaining allows them to improve their "batting average" and avoid trials which, in addition to consuming great amounts of time and requiring much work, can result in acquittals (Blumberg, 1967, p. 179). District attorneys who repeatedly lose cases might find their jobs in jeopardy. The public may be disturbed by the funds expended on the cases as well as the release of defendants who they view suspiciously. Individuals who are exonerated at trials may further damage the image of prosecutors, who may be viewed as picking on innocent citizens. In a system that places more value on convictions than actual sentences, prosecutors can easily view plea bargaining as a way to increase their conviction rates while avoiding potential problems (Kunkle, 1989).

Many private defense attorneys maximize their efficiency and profit through careful use of plea bargaining since it requires less time and effort than a full trial (Knowles & Prewitt, 1969; Moran & Cooper, 1983, p. 75). Clients are often unaware of the "worth of a case" and hire counsel in the belief that they will get them the best deal. Many attorneys, in fact, specialize in bargains and are hired for this expertise rather than any courtroom skill (Moran & Cooper, 1983, p. 75).[3]

Private attorneys who acquiesce to the goal of the courtroom work group may be granted favors by prosecutors and judges, while those who take up court time and demand trials may be penalized. Preferential scheduling of their cases allows attorneys to maximize the use of their time and accept more clients. The granting of continuances helps attorneys collect fees from defendants who will not pay once the case is decided (Blumberg, 1967, p. 114). Scheduling of cases before a "favorable" judge can improve attorneys' reputations and fatten their fees (Blumberg, 1967, p. 105).

Prosecutors also may favor compliant counsel. For one, they may lower charges against certain defendants who are particularly important to the business of helpful attorneys. Recalcitrant counsel, on the other hand, may find that they are granted no favors. Quite the contrary, judges may vent their feelings toward such attorneys with longer sentences for their clients. This system of incentives and disincentives "coaxes" defense attorneys into cooperation.

Public defenders are not immune from the courtroom work groups' pressures to utilize plea bargains to speed cases along. The publicly appointed attorneys have sizable caseloads in urban centers and in order to manage their work must carefully select only a few cases for trial. The counsel are part of the system. They daily talk and socialize with other members of the courtroom scene including prosecutors and judges. The defendants are outsiders whose presence in the court will last only minutes. It should not be surprising that the attorneys serve the system's rather than their clients' needs (Blumberg, 1967, pp. 114–115).

OUTSIDE INFLUENCES ON THE COURTROOM WORKGROUP

The court work group's goal of expeditiously disposing of cases is affected by "outside" groups. The media may expose the darker side of plea bargaining to the public. For some of the audience, the decreased penalties afforded defendants who bargain is enough reason to terminate the courtroom ritual. At the other end of the spectrum, there are those who detest the trampling of individual rights in favor of bureaucratic efficiency.

Appellate decisions also play some role in lower court behavior. If the work group were to simply sanction defendants for refusing to cooperate with internal norms, due process would suffer. This would certainly attract attention and restrictive action by the appellate courts and professional groups (for example, bar associations) that monitor qualitative aspects of the work group's procedures (Nardulli, 1978, p. 76). Besides, judges do not like to have cases overturned due to errors they made while the cases were in their courts. It is a public announcement of their mistakes; mistakes that may have released criminals back into society.

The state legislature also influences the work group through its ability to pass criminal laws, set minimum sentences, and enact legislation that controls the functioning of the court itself. The best illustration of such activities is Alaska's legislative ban on plea bargaining in criminal courts. But, other laws often indirectly affect the plea bargaining process. Mandated jail terms for convictions for certain offenses removes the possibility of bargaining with respect to punishment for these offenses. Rather, the negotiations between the courtroom group center on the charges to which defendants will eventually plead guilty. For example, defendants may be allowed to plead guilty to reckless driving rather than be charged with drunk driving, which often carries mandated penalties.

Local political parties, civic reform groups, and quasi-governmental watchdog agencies act as additional monitors on the operations of the court work group (Nardulli, 1978, pp. 75–76). Inadequate attention to conviction rates, statistics regarding case dispositions, or severity of sentences may likely result in media exposes and recall elections. If murderers, rapists, and robbers received ridiculously low sentences in order to persuade them to plead guilty, the public would certainly be outraged. Therefore, the courtroom work group cannot dispose of its cases by simply lowering the price of crime until defendants accept the sentencing offer. Public outrage would also result if those convicted of minor offenses after jury trials were sentenced too harshly for resisting the work group's norms. It is for this reason, that while the decision to exercise one's right to trial must involve some cost to ensure cooperation, that cost cannot be too high (Nardulli, 1978, pp. 74–76).

Organizational theory indicates that to study sentencing adequately, researchers must consider the identity and strength of the work groups involved in disposing of the cases under study. Sentencing decisions, although they rest with judges, are controlled by concerns of the three members of the courtroom elite. Other characteristics of the defendants may have little effect on sentencing once one controls for the severity of the offense and the identity of the work group.

Organizational theory, however, does not fully explain sentencing in judicially dominated situations. Assigning judges a half-hearted role in sentencing downplays their importance in circumstances where other members of the courtroom work group are not present or play minimal roles. While plea bargaining is often controlled by prosecutors and defense attorneys, sentencing in municipal courts may be minimally affected by factors posited as important by organizational theorists. Offenders in misdemeanor criminal cases, for example, are seldom represented by counsel and plea bargaining may not be important in minor offenses (Mileski, 1971). Prosecutors also are sometimes absent from traffic courts (Brickey & Miller, 1975).

Low visibility of municipal tribunals is related to the "highly discretionary brand of justice" found in the lower courts (Bartollas et al., 1983, p. 131). Judges may view due process rules as obstacles and only follow them when an appeal is possible (Mileski, 1971, p. 486). Record keeping at the municipal court level, however, is often irregular and inadequate (Ashman, 1975, p. 31). Transcripts are seldom made due to the absence of court reporters. Even simple records regarding which defendants appeared in court and the outcomes of the hearings are often not kept. As a result, lower court decisions are seldom appealed, and the routines established in them may continue undisturbed (Mileski, 1971, p. 518). Lacking other work group members or outside influences, the judges are free to determine penalties.

VARIETY OF SANCTIONS AVAILABLE

Misdemeanor courts may "experiment with a wide variety of sanctions" since they hear less serious cases (Ragona & Ryan, 1983, p. 199). The punishments employed by the misdemeanor courts include many of those found in the higher criminal courts: fines, probation, and incarceration. The misdemeanor courts, however, also routinely sentence offenders to community service, placement in rehabilitation-oriented institutions such as alcohol or drug treatment centers, required attendance in education programs, mandatory counseling, and restitution.

The felony courts do not share the lower tribunal's ability to utilize a broad assortment of sanctions with great discretion. Sentencing in federal and many state courts, for example, is now accomplished through utilization of strict sentencing guidelines, where each legal factor in a case (for example, type of offense, harm to victim, monetary damage, offender's role in the crime, number and type of priors) contributes to a narrowly defined sentence.

Fines are the most common sanction utilized by the lower criminal courts. More than 40 percent of sentenced offenders receive only a fine as punishment and an equal amount are sentenced to a fine plus probation or jail (Ryan, 1980–81; Ragona & Ryan, 1983; Feeley, 1979; Lindquist, 1988, p. 26; President's Commission Task Force Report on the Courts, 1967, p. 18). It is this phenomenon that lead one expert (Mileski, 1971, p. 501) to note that "offenders must pay in dollars more often than in days in all offense categories."

Jail sentences are rarely imposed in cases at the misdemeanor level, but there are considerable variations from court to court. Studies of the subject indicate that the percentage of convicted offenders sent to jail range from less than 5 percent of misdemeanants in one lower court (Feeley, 1979, p. 137) to a high of 35 percent in another district (Ryan, 1980–81, see also Mileski, 1971). Judges, in general, feel few criminals should go to jail and cite several reasons for their belief: costs to society, loss of defendants' freedom, possible rape and/or injury of defendants while in jail, and loss of taxes on defendants' income (Wice, 1985, p. 150).

Imposition of jail sentences may also be affected by external limitations. Increased criminalization of behaviors have combined with harsher penalties to overfill our jails. Taxpayers, however, have been somewhat reluctant to approve the funds to build new facilities. Moreover, they have ferociously fought attempts to place county jails in their neighborhoods. The few new jails that have been built have done little to alleviate the cramped conditions. An increasing number of jurisdictions have been ordered by higher courts to lessen their jail populations. Shorter terms result because prisoners in these counties must be released to make room for incoming captives.

Judges are aware of the burgeoning jail overcrowding and divert some offenders to less restrictive punishments. Municipal court judges have recently adopted community service as a sanction. Although utilized somewhat in colonial Boston (sentencing drunkards to chop wood) and in the South (chain gangs building highways), modern community service began in Alameda County, California, during the mid-1960s (Klein, 1988, p. 175). County judges did not want to sentence female traffic offenders to jail and opted to place them in community agencies as volunteers.

A decision (*Tate v. Short*) handed down by the U.S. Supreme Court in 1971 prohibiting the incarceration of indigent offenders for an inability to pay fines fueled the use of community service. The benefits are many: the community profits from the labor of the offender, who may learn basic work skills or discipline, and jail overcrowding is not increased (Klein, 1988, pp. 173, 174, 178).

By 1976, over 4,500 offenders had been placed by the Alameda County court system (Klein, 1988, p. 175). Use of community service sentences then spread to other regions of the nation and elsewhere. Officials from New York, for example, visited Great Britain in 1976, observed the British community service program, and decided to implement their own program (Klein, 1988, p. 176).

Community service sentences are used by the courts in place of fines or jail for nonserious offenses (for example, shoplifting and disorderly conduct) and can involve a variety of tasks. Community service placement sites are usually with nonprofit or governmental agencies. Typical community service sites in one California county included youth and charitable organizations, homes for the elderly or handicapped individuals, recycling centers, schools, parks, and libraries; typical tasks involved "maintenance, clerical work, or assisting others" (Meeker et al., 1992, p. 200). One expert noted:

> Community service is viewed by some as a panacea: Unlike the more traditional probation conditions which are based on the offender refraining from doing something negative such as committing a new crime, community work service orders require the offender to do something positive. They are easily measurable and enforced. The sanction is almost excuse proof, as indigence is not a bar to its completion. In fact, unemployed

offenders have more time to complete work service hours. . . . Further, there is consistently enthusiastic public support for such sentences. Not only does the public understand that the offender is being required to make up for the crime, it actually sees the results in terms of repainted fire hydrants, cleaned beaches, dusted library books, and so on. (Klein, 1988, p. 187)

Estimates indicate, for example, that community service workers provide the California transit authority in Los Angeles and Ventura counties free labor worth more than $30 million each year (Webber & Nikos, 1992).

In some jurisdictions, an argument has developed between the courts and service agencies. Many local government agencies desire the large revenues the lower courts generate through the collection of fines (Ashman, 1975, p. 16; Lindquist, 1988, p. 24; President's Commission Task Force Report on the Courts, 1967, p. 35). Since the imposition of community service sentences decreases monetary penalties, arguments have developed between agencies and government over their use. In California's San Fernando Valley, for example, the application of community service penalties has recently decreased, probably to help meet budgetary problems faced by the courts (Stevenson, 1993). Only truly indigent offenders now qualify for the alternative punishment in lieu of fines, leading to heavy financial penalties for many offenders who would have been given the option of community service. The government and nonprofit agencies where offenders had completed their sentences have felt the crunch due to this new policy. These agencies are less able to perform their duties effectively as fewer and fewer offenders are available to help.

The situation in the San Fernando Valley demonstrates that sentences in municipal courts are open to influence from other than legal variables. Budget problems, jail overcrowding, or local sentencing preferences may all influence how sentences are imposed. These external limitations may vary from county to county and, therefore, affect sentencing in distinct ways based on local conditions. They establish an accepted range of sanctions in which judges are free to determine sentences. Variation among the judges within this range is based on individual differences, such as judicial punishment philosophy.

Community service sentences are open to judicial bias since they are discretionary. They were meant to be biased in some group's favor. Judges in Alameda County, for example, sentenced some female traffic offenders to community service, but males, who committed similar offenses, did jail time. To this point, one study (Meeker, Jesilow, & Aranda, 1992) found that Hispanics and males were more likely to be sentenced to pick up trash along freeways as their community service placements, while whites and women were sent to more pleasant surroundings, such as libraries, hospitals, and parks.

CONCLUSIONS

It is likely that sentences are based on a wide array of factors; some are legal characteristics such as the severity of the crimes or offenders' prior criminal records; some are extralegal characteristics of the defendants (ethnicity or gender, for example); others may be matters connected to individual judges (for example, their philosophies of punishment).

The concern of many in our society is that individual philosophies and biases of judges will lead them to punish some offenders more severely than others who commit similar crimes. Judges, for example, occasionally dismiss minor offenses committed by college students so they avoid the stigmas of convictions (Feeley, 1979, p. 23). Inequities resulting from judicial bias can undermine public trust in the criminal justice system; in particular, minorities might perceive the courts as part of an oppressive structure. Such fears have led many to look for evidence of judicial favoritism. The next chapter reviews the literature with respect to bias in judicial sentencing, paying particular attention to the methodological difficulties of such research.

CHAPTER 2

RESEARCH ON BIAS IN JUDICIAL SENTENCING

A great deal of research has been conducted to determine whether and under what circumstances extralegal factors, such as race and gender, affect the severity of criminal sentences handed out by judges. Most of these studies, however, have depended more on increasing sophistication in research methodologies and/or statistical techniques than well-formed research plans. Although academic research necessarily involves building on earlier works and increasing sophistication as improved methods become available, the research on judicial bias in sentencing can best be described as a methodological battle that has intensified with each new publication. Researchers appear to react to the work of others in the field by submitting a study that is "superior," due to more sophisticated methods or a better choice of variables.

JUDICIAL BIAS

In 1764, in the publication of the first edition of *Dei delitti e delle pene* (An Essay on Crimes and Punishments), Cesare Beccaria (1775/1983) noted that decisions by judges do not always reflect the legal merits of the case. He argued that justice often meant judicial favoritism; the powerful met with favor from the courts while the powerless met with severe sanctions.

Beccaria felt that the purpose of punishment should be to prevent people from committing crimes. Among other reforms, Beccaria (1775/1983) argued for certainty and swiftness of punishment, knowledge of the laws by the citizenry, revision of the sentencing structure to reflect the severity of each crime, and replacement of the practice of judges determining punishments with one in which punishments are set by legislators. The judiciary, he believed, with their many deeply rooted biases and varying punishments, were unable to implement his philosophy of deterrence. Beccaria (1775/1983, p. 5) noted that justice suffered when judges set sentences according to whim:

> The spirit of the laws will then be the result of the good, or bad logic of the judge; and this will depend on his good or bad digestion; on the violence of his passions; on the rank, and condition of the accused, or on his connections with the judge; and on all those little circumstances, which change the appearance of objects in the fluctuating mind of man.

By allowing sentences to be set by judges, Beccaria (1775/1983, p. 5) argued, differences result that cannot be explained through legal reasoning: "We see the same crimes punished in a different manner at different times in the same tribunals."

The dilemma of judicial bias did not end with Beccaria's comments, of course. Throughout American history, judges have been accused of discrimination; for the most part for sentencing nonwhites more severely than whites. Such judicial bias during earlier times may have been based on institutionalized differences between whites and their former slaves. For example, the United States Supreme Court in *Plessy v. Ferguson* (1896) held that courts could not be expected to guarantee equality to blacks: "If one race be inferior to the other socially, the Constitution of the United States cannot put them upon the same plane."[1]

Some early laws were designed to sentence black offenders more harshly than whites. An 1848 Virginia statute, for example, required the death penalty for any offense committed by a black that could result in three or more years in prison for a white (Jones, 1981, p. 543). Blacks sentenced under this statute could be expected to receive harsher sentences than their white counterparts, but this was hardly due only to individual judicial biases. Other laws of the nation also treated whites differently from minorities under at least some circumstances (see for example, *Brown v. Board of Education,* 1954; *Gong Lum v. Rice,* 1927; *McLaughlin v. Florida,* 1964). Judges could not ignore race when determining sentences in such instances.

Despite discriminatory laws and acts, the courts have clung to the notion of equality connoted by the image of Lady Justice in her blindfold, holding a scale that allows only legal evidence to tip the pans in favor of the state; a trusting faith that the powerful and the powerless stand as equals before the law. It is clear that most actions by judges are not biased. In actuality, it is likely that few official judicial acts involve any form of extralegal prejudice against minorities.

Yet, examples of individual judicial bias do exist. In one instance, in sentencing a Spanish-surnamed defendant to death, the judge referred to him as a "cold-blooded, copper-colored, blood-thirsty, throat-cutting, chili-eating, sheep-herding, murdering son-of-a-bitch" (*United States v. Gonzales,* 1881, as reprinted in Inciardi, 1990, p. 491). The question is not whether bias exists in the court system, but rather what kinds of biases exist, under what circumstances are they maximized, and under what situations are they minimized.

POSSIBLE SOURCES OF BIAS

There are many potential sources of extralegal bias in the judicial system. Those that have received the most attention in the criminal justice literature are race/ethnicity, socioeconomic status, gender, and age. Other factors that have been examined include type of legal counsel available to defendants, whether or not the defendants are detained before trial, and the strength of the cooperation between judge, prosecutor, and defense attorney.

The race or ethnicity of the defendant is the most often researched demographic factor related to sentencing and certainly the most controversial. The race/ethnicity debate has focused, for the most part, on whether blacks are treated more harshly at sentencing than whites. The argument, as noted earlier, has become an escalating methodological fight in which researchers denounce each other's work in a game of academic one-upmanship.

The first empirical examination of racial bias, published in 1928 by Thorsten Sellin, concluded that blacks were discriminated against at the trial and sentencing stages. According to his comparisons of government records of conviction rates and sentences during 1926 in Detroit, blacks were more likely to be convicted and more likely to be harshly punished. Sellin based his conclusions on the percentage of arrests that resulted in convictions for nineteen different crimes, ranging from begging and vagrancy to murder. For eleven of the offenses, blacks were more likely than whites to be convicted.[2]

Sellin (1928) argued that, once convicted, blacks were sentenced more harshly than whites, noting that 30.9% of black felons received a jail sentence compared with only 15.5% of the whites. This finding, however, as Sellin (1928, p. 59) pointed out, may be an artifact of the higher number of "serious offenses calling for heavier penalties" committed by blacks. If offenses of a graver nature resulted in harsher sentences, the resulting disparities cannot be alone attributed to racial biases.

By basing conviction rates on the number of suspects arrested, Sellin unintentionally introduced many factors associated with the police (e.g., arrest policy) that likely distorted his conviction rates for both blacks and whites. Sellin recognized that the conviction rates may have been affected by "unwarranted arrests of Negroes" (p. 59) that resulted from broad sweeps in which police arrested blacks on "the flimsiest charges" (p. 54).On the one hand as unreasonable arrests increased, the conviction rate may have decreased as the courts dismissed those cases that involved little or no evidence against defendants. Groundless arrests of either race would naturally deflate the conviction rates when those defendants were released. Expenditure of greater resources to police a particularly crime-ridden area, on the other hand, would result in more arrests based on solid evidence, which would likely increase the conviction rates.

The judicial bias reported by Sellin may be attributed, at least in part, to the police who made the arrests. Police policy, then, could affect conviction rates regardless of how judges treat the cases at later stages in the justice system. This may explain why statistics for a sizable minority (7) of the eighteen crimes indicated that convictions were more likely for whites. Whites were likely arrested only when strong evidence warranted it, which lead to higher conviction rates for them.

Another important factor to consider when interpreting Sellin's (1928) findings centers on reduced charges. Because of discretion exercised by prosecutors before trial or by justices or juries at the judgment stage, convictions do not always reflect the offenses for which the perpetrators were arrested. Degrees of offenses may be lowered, defendants may be acquitted of some charges but not others, charges may be dropped, or charges may be transformed altogether. Due to weak evidence, defendants arrested for burglary under this scenario may be convicted of trespassing. This phenomenon may well taint Sellin's data. While only three blacks were arrested for manslaughter/negligent homicide, for example, ten were convicted of this offense. Some of these convictions, of course, were for offenses other than those for which the defendants were arrested. Assuming this is true for other offenses indicates that the reported conviction rates may be incorrect.

Sellin's early inquiry did not report the statistical significance of his findings. By today's research standards, Sellin's determination of which of the two rates was higher would not be sufficient to support his conclusions that bias exists. Indeed, the differences were not always large; discrepancies for six out of eighteen[3] offenses were less than 2.2 percent. His figures for assault and battery, for example, yielded a discrepancy of one-tenth of 1 percent (49.0 percent for blacks versus 48.9 percent for whites), hardly a meaningful difference.

Another concern with the validity of Sellin's findings stems from his use of government data. The manner in which information is collected is of interest to researchers. Data can be gathered from existing records (usually government statistics) or they can be collected by researchers through observations. Official records are usually much easier to obtain both in terms of time and money. Collecting original data may sometimes entail difficulties in gaining access to certain information that may be of interest to researchers. Defendants' prior records, for example, strongly influence penalties (Chiricos & Bales, 1991; Gordon & Glaser, 1991; Green, 1961, p. 98; Gottfredson, 1978/1981; Lemert & Rosberg, 1948; Meeker, Jesilow & Aranda, 1992; Myers, 1987; Petersilia & Turner, 1985; Pommersheim & Wise, 1989; Spohn, 1990; Zatz, 1985), but is often treated as confidential information by the system.

Analysis of existing records necessarily limits the information researchers may consider to those items that were originally recorded, and usually researchers wish to consider at least one tidbit that was not collected. Further, researchers must accept existing records in whatever form they appear, although they may be incomplete, incorrect, or biased. To this end, Sellin (1928, p. 54) very appropriately noted, "The records of our police departments, our courts, and our penal institutions have not been compiled to suit the purposes of criminological research."

Sellin (1928) was obliged to accept the data as complete and correct, free from any biases. As indicated by the figures for manslaughter, which indicate that more blacks were convicted than arrested, it is readily apparent that errors crept into the data, a problem Sellin recognized. For example, he was unable to offer a clear interpretation of a government table that showed types of sentences by race:

> The study from which this table has been compiled does not indicate the exact meaning of the data presented in this column or the process by which they were secured. I assume these figures represent minimum and maximum sentences; the heading is far from clear. (Sellin, 1928, p. 61)

More than forty years later, a court expert (Mileski, 1971) argued that inaccuracies in data were sometimes due to workgroups' efforts to protect themselves and their sentencing practices from scrutiny. This self-protecting behavior led to omissions in the data that were more than simply convenient; bureaucrats cataloged a host of factors that show judges in a good light while ignoring many important factors that more accurately represented how judges sentenced.

Another notable methodological problem with Sellin's attempt to study judicial bias was that his data very likely included cases where juries, rather than judges, determined the final sentences. Penalties in murder cases, for example, are often set by juries that decide if offenders are executed or spend their lives in prison. Early researchers did not report who set the sentences that they studied and labeled as biased, either due to a lack of interest in the matter or, more likely, because of an inability to tease this information out of existing governmental records. It is very likely that at least some of the punishments in the early studies were ordered by juries. If bias appears in sentences set by juries, it is more an indicator of the inadequacies of the jury system (or portions thereof, such as the lack of instructions given to guide the jurors in the task of setting sentences) than a demonstration of judicial bias.[4]

It is difficult to determine whether or not Sellin's (1928) findings can be cited as evidence of racial bias in sentencing. Questionable data combined with unsophisticated methods and conflicting results make this article very difficult to depend on as irrefutable evidence of bias.[5]

RACIAL DYADS

The 1940s saw the introduction of a new method for studying judicial bias. In 1941, Guy Johnson introduced the concept of victim-offender dyads as a determining factor in severity of sentences. Johnson argued that a "caste definition of crime" defined offenses against whites as more serious than offenses against blacks:

Obviously the murder of a white person by a Negro and the murder of a Negro by a Negro are not at all the same kind of murder from the standpoint of the upper caste's scale of values, yet in crime statistics they are thrown together. (Johnson, 1941, p. 98)

Johnson (1941, p. 101) found that, for his sample, blacks who killed whites were more likely to be convicted and punished severely, while numerous blacks who murdered other blacks "probably go unpunished or are punished" lightly. Johnson concluded that victim-offender dyads impacted sentences because intragroup homicides by blacks did not disturb white majority group members, while homicides of other whites did.

Harold Garfinkel (1949), after examining court records and death certificates in North Carolina, explained that the criminality of blacks who killed other blacks had to be deter- mined by a trial, while the criminality of blacks accused of killing whites was determined (or rather assumed) from the outset. Blacks who killed other blacks were presumed innocent until proven guilty, while blacks who killed whites were assumed guilty even before trial.

Later researchers were not prepared to accept the victim-offender dyad results reported by Johnson (1941) and Garfinkel (1949) as proof of racial bias by judges or the criminal justice system. Edward Green (1964, p. 358), for example, argued that the circumstances of crimes committed by blacks against whites were more serious; that is, such crimes were "of a more aggravated nature, indicating a deeper internalization of the value of violence," while crimes by blacks against blacks were "high in impulsiveness and low in . . . malicious intent." The seriousness of the actual offense, then, explained for Green why blacks received harsher treatment in the courts.

Two methodological problems with respect to judicial bias that plagued Sellin also faced Johnson (1941) and Garfinkel (1949): questions regarding who ordered the punishments and a lack of statistical sophistication. Since both Johnson (1941) and Garfinkel (1949) studied murder cases, it is probable that juries, not judges, determined guilt and penalties. Both studies were conducted in states where murder trials were often heard by juries (Johnson's study included cases from Virginia, North Carolina, and Georgia; Garfinkel's from

North Carolina). Garfinkel (1949, p. 373) noted, for example, that North Carolina rules of trial procedure forbade trial by judge unless the defendant pleaded guilty to some murder less than first degree and then only to determine the appropriate punishment (Garfinkel, 1949, p. 373).

Further eroding the attribution of bias to the judges in Johnson's (1941) and Garfinkel's (1949) work was a North Carolina statute that mandated the death penalty for defendants convicted of first-degree murder. Under such circumstances it is probably more valid to ascribe the bias to prosecutors who chose the charges to be levied against defendants. Prosecutors are usually conceded to be the most powerful actors in the criminal justice drama since they may without official review choose to include or drop charges.

The other methodological mystery with Johnson's (1941) and Garfinkel's studies (1949) is the exclusion of significance levels for their statistics. Without such information, we are left to guess if their results were merely a chance conclusion created by the sample they chose to study or likely valid representations of sentencing.[6] Both authors used simple comparisons of percentages. Although their comparisons may have appealed to the uninitiated reader of yesterday, contemporary research audiences demand more sophistication before accepting a study's results. The extent of bias ascribed to judges in these studies must be suspect.

FURTHER REFINEMENTS

In their examination of the courts, Edwin Lemert and Judy Rosberg (1948) were the first widely published researchers to include tests of significance in their findings. They criticized prior research that did not consider the defendants' prior criminal records. Evidence of continuing illegal activity, they posited, was important in judicial decision making. Their work, for example, indicated that defendants with prior records were less likely to receive probation and that defendants with no previous criminal convictions were seldom sent to prison. The types of illegalities for which defendants had previously been sentenced also swayed their punishments. Judges, as with the rest of us, mentally rank criminal past activities in terms of items considered important: Was anybody injured? Was there the potential for serious harm? How much money was stolen? Serious prior records influenced judges to dispense harsher sentences.

Lemert and Rosberg (1948) noted that whites, on the one hand, were convicted of less dangerous offenses: grand thefts, second-degree burglaries, and victimless crimes. Minorities, on the other hand, were more likely to have prior felonies for potentially grave actions such as assaults with deadly weapons. Whites and minorities convicted of similar offenses might possess widely differing past criminal records, and the appearance of judicial bias in early studies might have been explained by this fundamental difference.

New Folly

A methodological message of Lemert's and Rosberg's work was that researchers had to expand the number of items they considered when attempting to extract the effect of bias from apparent sentencing disparities. Judicial decisions were based on several matters and research efforts should reflect their complexity. With this in mind, Henry Bullock (1961) collected information on race, type of offense, previous felonies, type of plea, county of residence and length of sentence for inmates in the Texas State Prison serving sentences for burglary, rape, and murder. He posited that studies that failed to control for these factors may "have derived conclusions concerning racial bias from comparisons of white and Negro subjects whose characteristics differed significantly in factors other than race" (p. 412).

Bullock's (1961) attempt to study bias was admirable. But, ironically, it failed to address adequately the most important issue: who was doing the sentencing. Bullock (1961, p. 412) refers to his work as a study of "bias at the judicial level," but he limited his research to offenders sentenced by juries. Nonetheless, Bullock's work is often cited in the judicial bias literature and is part of the foundation on which later studies were built (Hagan, 1974; Hagan & Bumiller, 1983).

Bullock's (1961) study served as one of many projects that fueled further conflict in the methodological battle to determine whether or not judicial bias existed. He was one of the first researchers to report the degree of the relationship between the severity of sentences handed out to offenders and other items. For example, he was able to indicate the strength of the association between the type of crime for which defendants were convicted and their punishments, not just that the two were related.[7]

Bullock (1961) reported that the severity of offenses, the extent of urbanization and region where the cases were heard, and the type of pleas defendants entered influenced the harshness of penalties.[8] As offense severity or degree of urbanization increased, so did length of sentence. Further, those who pleaded not guilty or were tried in East Texas received longer sentences than those who pleaded guilty or were tried in West Texas.

The importance of Bullock's (1961) research lays not in his findings, but in the trend he started. Later researchers further refined the factors Bullock had believed contributed to punishment severity and included them in their studies. Bullock's "degree of urbanization" measure (which he based on whether the county contained at least one large city) is certainly a precursor to later use of ecological variables to determine effects of community context on sentencing by judges (e.g., Myers, 1987).

Bullock's (1961) research sheds little light on judicially ordered penalties since he surveyed only offenders sentenced by juries, but some of his results may be applicable to judges. Findings, for example, indicating that the length of punishments are affected by the severity of offenses are apt to generalize to judges because of the similarities between them and juries. Criminal court justices and jurors are usually drawn from local communities and, in theory, represent the community. Since both reflect the local sentiment to some degree, the level of disgust felt toward criminal offenses should be similar.[9]

DIFFERENCES IN CRIMINALITY

In his review of studies on sentencing, Edward Green (1961) noted several methodological concerns. For one, he criticized the lack of adequate controls for prior record (p.10). The total number of felony convictions offenders had accumulated, Green hypothesized, would likely have more effect on the punishments ordered by judges than simply knowing that the defendants had committed prior felonies. He chastised some researchers for their use of poor data and addressed the inadequate statistical controls used by others:

> Thus the complexity of the sentencing process, not to mention the process of human judgement, has been all but submerged in simplistic interpretations based upon fragmentary data. The neglect, in comparing the sentences of various groups of cases, to impose statistical controls appropriate to the subject of inquiry has resulted in a circularity of reasoning—the lack of proper and uniform criteria for sentencing is inferred from the disparities in sentences; and these in turn are attributed to the lack of adequate criteria. (Green, 1961, p. 20)

In order to address these concerns, Green (1961, p. 21) examined a sample of cases heard in a "non-jury prison court" of the Philadelphia Court of Quarter Sessions during 1956 and 1957. His study is significant for two major reasons. First, he limited it to sentences imposed by judges. Second, Green considered three types of factors that may affect the severity of punishments ordered by judges: legal, extralegal, and process related.

Legal matters, for Green, included the types and number of offenses for which the defendants were being sentenced, their prior criminal records, and official recommendations to the court that appear in presentence and neuropsychiatric reports. Extralegal (or "legally irrelevant") characteristics of the offenders included their gender, age, race, and place of birth. Process related items were factors associated with the dispositions of the cases: whether the defendants pled guilty, or were represented by private or public counsel, and individual differences of the judges and prosecutors.

Green (1961) found that the types of crimes offenders committed were the primary determinants of the severity of their punishments; the more physical harm caused to victims, the harsher the penalties. The next important sentencing criterion was the number of instant offenses for which defendants were convicted; the higher the number, the more severe the sentences. The extent of defendants' prior records was the third factor that explained sentence severity; as the number of prior offenses increased, so did the harshness of the punishments imposed by the judges. Finally, the recency of the defendants prior convictions ranked fourth in explaining sentence severity; the more recent the convictions, the harsher the penalties.

Extralegal and process related matters (except for minor property offenses[10]) did not appear to affect the sentences that the judges ordered once other matters, such as prior records, were taken into consideration. Green (1961) concluded that previously observed sentence disparities were not based on judicial bias:

> To sum up, the results provide assurance that the deliberations of the sentencing judge are not at the mercy of his passions or prejudices but comply with the mandate of the law. The criteria for sentencing recognized in the law, the nature of the crime and the offender's prior criminal record, are the decisive determinants of the severity of the sentence. (p. 102)

ORGANIZATIONAL THEORISTS: THE COURTROOM WORK GROUP

Abraham Blumberg (1967) was one of the first researchers to argue that the organization of the courts affected judicial decision making. Earlier work "virtually ignored" the reality that the court system operates much like other organizations with a "community of human beings who are engaged in doing certain things with, to, and for each other" (Blumberg, 1967, p. ix). The mutual cooperation between the key players in the court system may explain what happens in court, including sentencing decisions by judges.

James Eisenstein and Herbert Jacob (1977, p. 10) maintained that those who form the "courtroom work group" (the judge, prosecutor, and defense attorney) are driven by "incentives and shared goals." Further, these organizational goals are more important than individual biases against any particular type of defendant (minorities, murderers, or recidivists, for example) when determining the severity of sentences handed out by judges.

Peter Nardulli (1978, p. 70) argued that the courtroom work group is composed of the judge, prosecutor, and defense attorney because "within the courtroom setting, these three individuals enjoy a virtual monopoly of power." According to Nardulli, members of the courtroom work group conduct their operations in a way that benefits both themselves and the group as a whole.

Nardulli (1978, p. 55) attributed the inadequacies of earlier researchers to their consideration of sentencing "in isolation from other stages in the dispositional process" and their ignorance of:

> [sentencing's] role within the court's overall dispositional strategy. This impeded their ability to validly assess the role of extraneous factors in criminal court sentencing. It also hampered their ability to identify sources of disparities in sentencing.

Nardulli (1978, p. 206) noted that researchers failed to include the interests of the work group who control and operate the courtroom processes. Considering their concerns, he argued, could "yield significant and unique contributions to the study of criminal courts" (Nardulli, 1978, p. 77).

The presence or absence of legal counsel is one of the situational variables important to those who study the effects of the courtroom work group on judicial sentencing. Some judges have been accused of a heavier hand with unrepresented defendants, presumably due to a number of matters. In the ideal, attorneys delineate their clients' concerns and safeguard their legal rights. They inform judges about mitigating factors that may be considered in the imposition of sentences. Some attorneys, because of their trial records or connections, benefit defendants when judges offer lenient sentences due to the attorneys' prestige, or cases are sometimes dismissed by the prosecution if defendants have "particularly adept" attorneys even if the evidence is strong (Mileski, 1971, p. 492). The presence or lack of an attorney, then, may affect judges' sentencing.

The type of counsel defendants obtain may affect their eventual punishments. For one, judges may sentence those represented by public defenders more harshly because they may view them as less competent than private counsel or believe public attorneys are less likely to appeal or publicize sentences. A court administrator, for example, posited that some black defendants in a large metropolitan area were at a disadvantage because their attorneys, public defenders, "are not considered 'real' lawyers by some, and as a result, . . . judges do not take defense arguments as seriously (Uhlman, 1979, p. 101)."

The addition of court-related items to the analyses greatly increased the number of factors to be considered in attempts to determine the influences on judges sentencing practices. Maureen Mileski (1971), for example, observed misdemeanor court proceedings and collected information on defendants' offenses and prior records as well as race, age, and gender. In addition, she noted if the defendants had attorneys and whether the attorneys were court appointed or privately employed; the defendants' pleas (guilty or not guilty); interactions between judges and defendants (whether they argued, or defendants offered excuses, or judges gave them instructions); and, the length of such discussions.

Mileski (1971) did not find support for the notion of a judicial bias against blacks. On the contrary, for at least one class of crimes—drunk in public, whites were more likely to be sentenced to jail. In place of jail, blacks were fined. Mileski (1971, p. 505) offered an explanation; whites who were intoxicated in public were more likely to be classified by the court-room work group as "skid row drunks"—older, homeless indigents who were nearly or already passed out. Drunk blacks, on the other hand, were more likely to be younger and employed, arrested because they were making noise on the street. The different sentences were explained by the different types of behaviors, not directly by their races. Mileski (1971, p. 508) noted that sentencing outcomes are the same for blacks and whites; "it is simply that proportionately more white defendants" are likely to be skid row drunks.[11]

Sentencing, argued Peter Nardulli (1978, p. 56), is the "most potent tool" for enforcing compliance with norms that allow the courtroom workgroup to operate expeditiously. Those defendants who frustrate the workgroup's efficiency are more harshly punished than those who cooperate. Nardulli reexamined existing data (Eisenstein & Jacob, 1977) on the sentencing decisions in 429 felonies processed in Chicago during 1972–73. Using a multiple regression equation, he concluded that penalties increased significantly for defendants who failed to cooperate with the courtroom work group. For example, a defendant who made one or no legal motions could expect a sentence of 25 months for armed robbery, while a similar defendant would receive a sentence of 64 months if he or she made between two and five motions. If the same defendant made more than five motions, he or she could expect a sentence of 102 months (1978, p. 216).[12]

James Eisenstein and Herbert Jacob (1977) also examined the effects of organizational factors on judicial sentencing. They interviewed members of courtroom work groups, observed cases, and collected case file data for a sample of felonies processed in Baltimore, Chicago, and Detroit during 1972. They decided that the identity of the courtroom work groups (i.e., which group processed the case) and the type of crimes for which they were convicted influenced decisions to send offenders to prison. Characteristics of the defendants did not appear to much affect the length of their imprisonments.[13]

Eisenstein and Jacob's (1977) study was not without its methodological problems. First, while they examined the "combined effects" of race, age, type of attorney, bail status, and prior record in their multivariate analysis, the authors did not discuss how the factors were combined to form this catchall variable. Prior record alone, for example, might have driven any relation, since numerous studies have found that it affects sentencing. They may have confounded their results further by categorizing prior record, traditionally considered a legal factor, as an extralegal characteristic. It is also possible that a single demographic factor (gender, e.g.) was related to the decision to imprison. In addition, some factors may have tended to increase sentences while others tended to decrease them, so that, in the final analysis, the individual factors may have canceled each other out, thereby resulting in "no effect." If prior record, for example, greatly influences sentences but gender and race only sometimes affect them, and then in different ways, then a construct including all three variables may appear to affect sentences in an irrational manner.

Eisenstein and Jacob's (1977) analysis signaled an end to bivariate research. Their employment of multivariate statistics allowed them to examine the "simultaneous" effects of several factors on sentence lengths and decisions to imprison offenders.[14] Earlier researchers had scrutinized the influence of one variable at a time. Multivariate methods were necessary, the authors said, to gain an accurate picture of courts' dispositions of cases. Eisenstein and Jacob (1977, p. 185) wrote:

> Felony dispositions result from a very complex set of social interactions. No single variable or factor can explain them. Consequently, we cannot simply classify dispositions according to race of defendants, their prior record, or their bail status, and expect to demonstrate a strong relationship. These characteristics—together with others—interact in complex ways to produce the final results.

By the time Eisenstein and Jacob's book was published, other researchers (e.g., Chiricos & Waldo, 1975) were also using multivariate methods, probably in large part due to the spread of computers and packaged statistical programs which facilitated sophisticated analyses.[15] As more and more studies employed complex models, other researchers also increasingly used multivariate models. In this tradition, bivariate analyses became less and less standard.

JOHN HAGAN'S WORK

The availability of computer assisted analyses altered the arena for the methodological fight over bias in judicial sentencing. John Hagan's excellent 1974 review on the effects of extralegal factors (race, socioeconomic status, age, and gender) on judicial sentencing drew the battle lines. Hagan noted that earlier research did not control for the effects of important legal factors or explain much of the variation in sentence severity. He was struck by the small magnitude of the relationships that had been observed. He calculated a measure of association (Goodman and Kruskal's tau-b) for studies that reported no such measures so that he could determine how well sentence severity was explained by the researchers' models.

Hagan concluded that while a number of relationships indicating bias were statistically significant, they told us very little about punishment decisions. He attributed some of the reported findings of significance in past studies to the large sample sizes that were often used in research on judicial bias. Statistical significance is relatively easily obtained with such studies. It is possible, for example, that a study of tens of thousands of offenders might reveal that a certain type of person paid, on average, one dollar less in fines. A statistical test might, for the most part, rule out the possibility that the finding was an anomaly associated with the sample. Such a result, however, is of little importance. Such minor differences (one dollar, when fines are often hundreds of dollars) are not the stuff on which to hang policy decisions.

Hagan also addressed the inconsistency of findings reported by researchers. While one study said that blacks were sentenced more harshly, another found that blacks were treated leniently. This problem, Hagan surmised, may be related to differences in the way each researcher defined short and long sentences and/or the lack of controls for appropriate legal factors, including the severity of offenders' crimes and their prior records. For ease of statistical analyses, data were often dichotomized (Bullock, 1961, e.g., classified sentences as less than 10 years or 10 years and longer). Differing definitions between researchers as to what signified a long versus short sentence, then, could easily influence findings and make results appear to fluctuate.

Many researchers, of course, were already doing what they could to avoid the problems Hagan raised. But his review should not be minimized. For at a time when many academics were rushing to analyze existing data sets with new statistical models, he stopped to address the methodological problems.

MORE ADVANCED MODELS

Theodore Chiricos and Gordon Waldo (1975) were among the first researchers studying judicial sentencing to put to use the increasingly sophisticated math models and statistical analyses. They collected government data for 17 different felonies committed between 1969 and 1973 in North Carolina, South Carolina, and Florida.[16] Rather than dichotomizing the data, sentence length was measured in months to preserve its continuous nature (life sentences were coded as 480 months). They also employed a stepwise multiple correlation model using seven variables (race, socioeconomic status, age, degree of urbanization, prior convictions, prior incarceration in a juvenile institution, and number of arrests) to predict sentence length in Florida.[17] Unlike simple correlations, the stepwise model establishes an order of importance for each factor.[18] Using this process, the authors decided that extralegal matters had little impact on sentencing.[19]

Alan Lizotte (1978) built on the work of Hagan (1974) and Chiricos and Waldo (1975). Using a sophisticated statistical technique, path analysis,[20] that allows consideration of the effects of many variables at once, he sought to show, among other things, that "judges and juries assign sentences along racial . . . lines due to prejudice and discrimination" (Lizotte,

1978, p. 564). Lizotte reanalyzed, from Nardulli's (1978) data, a sample of 816 cases processed by the Chicago trial courts in 1971 and 1972.

Lizotte's (1978) first model hypothesized relationships between eight variables[21] and the length of offenders' sentences. The analysis looked for relationships between race[22] and (1) sentence length, (2) prior arrests, (3) bail amount, (4) ability to post bail, (5) offense seriousness, and (6) extent of evidence. Lizotte's analysis did not establish a direct path between race and sentence length. In his study, inability to make bail, in turn, lead to longer estimated prison sentences. Lizotte concluded that black defendants, after considering the other factors, were 16 percent less likely to make bail than whites. He calculated that the sentences of blacks were approximately four months longer than those of whites because of their financial inability to make bail.[23]

Lizotte (1978) recognized that his findings were far from proof of racial bias in judicial sentencing. Rather, his "model is meant to show the complicated interweaving of extralegal and legal characteristics and how they determine criminal sentencing." He argued, "[t]o view class-based extralegal characteristics of defendants as the prime mover in the criminal justice system would be as naive as claiming that they have no effect at all on criminal sanctioning" (1978, p. 578).

Combining Models

Thomas Uhlman (1977; 1979) noted that earlier researchers had tested three hypothesized models with respect to judicial bias: (1) blacks are sentenced more harshly than whites because their offenses are more serious (criminality); (2) blacks are treated harsher because they are poor (class status); and, (3) blacks are discriminated against because of their race (racism). Uhlman argued that to fully understand the influence of race on sentence, researchers must consider the three models jointly. Whatever relationship remained after the criminality and class status models "had the chance to operate" could be classified as due to racism (Uhlman, 1977, p. 31).

To test his theory, Uhlman (1977; 1979) obtained official sentencing data for 34,258 black and 9,344 white defendants who appeared in a large metropolitan trial court between 1968 and 1974. He performed two separate analyses. He first determined if there was a relationship between the type of offenses defendants committed, and (1) their likelihood of being convicted, (2) their likelihood of being sent to prison, and (3) the length of their sentences (in months). Based on his analysis, Uhlman (1979, p. 78) reported that blacks were punished more severely than whites for fifteen of sixteen crimes, ranging from gambling to murder, and that blacks were twice as likely than their white counterparts to receive prison sentences. He did not, however, find evidence that blacks were substantially more likely than whites to be convicted.[24]

Uhlman's (1977; 1979) second analysis used path analyses designed to measure the effects of the three models (criminality, class status, and racism) on the length of defendants' sentences. He also measured the effects of (1) the types of defendants' offenses, (2) the seriousness of their acts, (3) the number of charges against them, (4) their bail amounts, (5) their pretrial status (in-custody or free), (6) the types of attorneys they had, (7) the types of pleas they made, and (8) any charge reductions. With his approach, Uhlman was able to attribute part of his finding that blacks were punished more severely than whites to the inability of blacks to secure adequate counsel or to make bail.

Uhlman (1977, p. 39; 1979, p. 92) did, however, find a direct path between race and sentences, indicating that blacks were sentenced more severely by judges simply because they were black, but this result did not go without self-criticism. He recognized that at least part of the "racism" findings may be associated with prior records or socioeconomic status, characteristics of the defendants he did not know. A prior record often results in longer sentences and poverty may make one unable to post bail. Indeed, blacks are more likely than whites to have prior convictions and be poor. Despite the sophistication of his analysis, Uhlman was plagued by the same methodological problem that had sickened Sellin (1928) fifty years earlier—those who had originally collected the data had not done so with his research in mind.

MEASUREMENT OF PRIOR RECORD

Researchers recognized that valid results could be obtained only if they paid much more attention to the quality of their data and measures. Sophisticated analyses cannot right flawed data. Consider prior record, a characteristic commonly shown to be associated with sentencing decisions.

Susan Welch and her associates (Welch, Gruhl & Spohn, 1984) noted that although many researchers included some measure of prior record in their analyses, they did so in varied ways. Some academics used arrests or felony arrests as evidence of criminal pasts, while other researchers required some form of conviction to establish a prior record for defendants (any conviction, a felony conviction, or number of felony convictions). Still other scholars limited their definition of a prior record to include only those who had been incarcerated. A few academics even used a four-point summary scale that incorporated the number of arrests, convictions, and prison terms. In all, Welch and associates (1984) identified eleven different ways prior record had been measured.

Welch and her colleagues (1984) examined whether or not the eleven measurements were interchangeable. To do so, they studied a sample of 2,600 male defendants who committed one of fourteen felonies and whose cases were processed in a large city in the northeastern United States between 1968 and 1979. The authors (Welch et al., 1984, pp. 219–220) concluded that the measures of prior record were not the same, and that "researchers who use misdemeanor or felony arrest as an indicator of prior record are tapping something very different from those who use some measure of incarceration." If researchers used arrests, they could easily conclude that prior records did not affect the likelihood of imprisonment or the severity of sentences. If they used a form of prior incarceration, on the other hand, their conclusions would be quite the opposite—that judges punished those with prior records more severely than those without criminal histories.

The authors (Welch et al., 1984) found that the measures of prior record affected the two races differently.[25] Whites who had already served time in prison, for example, were 17 percent more likely to be sent back there than whites who had not previously served prison terms. For blacks, however, the difference was less; blacks who had served a prior prison term were 10 percent more likely to be reincarcerated than blacks who had never been to prison. Welch and her associates (1984) concluded that researchers should use a measure of prior record that reflects some form of incarceration because such measures consistently had effects on blacks and whites and were most associated with the severity of defendants' punishments.

Effect of Sentencing Guidelines on Minorities

Certainly, by the mid-1970s there was no indisputable evidence that judges were biased against blacks or any other group. But, there was plenty of anecdotal evidence that some offenders were not getting a fair shake in their prison sentences and that the cause was indeterminate sentencing (e.g., Frankel, 1973). The philosophy that criminals could be rehabilitated had led legislatures to enact indeterminate sentences for offenses (MacNamara, 1977). A robber, for example, might expect to receive a sentence of one year to life, allowing a parole board to decide later the exact moment of release. Some offenders, however, ended up serving long sentences for minor offenses when their parole boards proved unforgiving or they "misbehaved" in prison. The resultant sentence inconsistencies combined with the perceived failure of rehabilitation to end crime led to a national refashioning of sentencing ideology (Selke, 1993; von Hirsch, 1981).

Sentencing guidelines are one way legislatures attempt to limit disparities in penalties due to racial or other biases. These mandated guidelines establish specific sentences based on characteristics of defendants' crimes (e.g., seriousness) and their criminal records. The enactment of the guidelines sparked a new round of research that no longer was obsessed with trying to universally prove or disprove racial bias. Rather, academics devised methodologies designed to answer specific questions.

"Racially Tainted" Criteria

One of the first questions investigators tackled was whether sentencing guidelines would eliminate racial disparities in punishments. Toward this end, Joan Petersilia and Susan Turner (1985) examined the effects of guidelines on the dispositions of 16,500 males sentenced to prison in California in 1980 for robbery, assault, burglary, theft, forgery, or drug possession. California's 1977 Determinate Sentencing Act had presumably limited judicial discretion and pushed judges to impose similar sentences on defendants convicted of similar offenses.

Petersilia's and Turner's results indicated that some of the criteria that were utilized to establish sentences were likely to be associated with one race or the other. Blacks, on the one hand, were more apt to be on probation or parole at the moment of their offenses, or injure their victims, or use weapons during the crimes; three matters that increase the length of defendants' sentences. On the other hand, alcoholism and drug abuse, two criteria used to determine the appropriateness of probation, were more likely to be found among white offenders. The authors concluded that the use of guidelines would not eradicate racial disparities in sentencing since the criteria that judges were to employ to establish penalties were "racially tainted" (Petersilia and Turner, 1985, p. 17).

Chicanos as a Distinct Group

Punishments ordered by judges following the passage of California's determinate sentencing law were also examined by Marjorie Zatz (1984). She posited that findings from earlier research may have been tainted because "Hispanics" were not included in the research samples.[26] Hispanics, she argued, are different from both whites and blacks. Research in areas where they form a sizable part of the population should include them as a third important group:

The vast majority of studies compare sentencing patterns either for Whites and Blacks or for Whites and the

ambiguous group "nonwhites." The former categoriza-
tion of race totally ignores the racial/ethnic minorities.
The latter assumes without any empirical basis that all
minorities are treated similarly, at least in comparison
with Whites. . . . inclusion of Hispanics in sentencing
research is critical. (Zatz, 1984, p. 148)

Zatz used an advanced multivariate statistical technique (ordinary least squares regression) to examine the length of prison
terms meted out to 4,729 Hispanics, whites, and blacks in California during 1978. She concluded that the prior criminal
records of Hispanics significantly influenced their sentences,
but they were relatively unimportant for whites or blacks. In
addition, judges generally penalized Hispanics who entered
"slow pleas" (instances where defendants, sometime after their
arraignments, change their initial pleas of not guilty to guilty)
more harshly than their white or black counterparts. Zatz concluded that Hispanics are treated differently from blacks and
whites by the courts and, therefore, should be viewed by
researchers as a distinct category instead of lumped together
with other minorities in white/nonwhite comparisons.

Ecological Variables

In the late 1980s researchers explored the possibility that
factors outside the courtroom might affect punishments
ordered by justices. In a district that is characterized by great
income inequality, for example, magistrates may severely punish property offenders in order to protect the interests of the
powerful, while intraclass assaults among the poor may be
lightly penalized because the powerful are unconcerned with
what happens in poverty neighborhoods. To examine such
notions, Martha Myers (1987; Myers & Talarico, 1988) introduced a number of ecological matters, such as a county's ethnic composition and income, into her research.

Myers examined the punishments ordered by Georgia
judges for 15,270 felons between 1976 and 1982.[27] Her analyses
indicated that harsher penalties for blacks were more com-

mon in areas characterized by greater income inequality.[28] In counties with a majority black population, however, blacks were treated with more favor; a situation Myers (1987, p. 761) attributed to the likely presence of a "relatively powerful black middle or upper-middle class" that may be less likely to condone racial bias. In areas with few blacks, however, this source of countervailing power may be nonexistent.

In an analogous study, George Bridges and colleagues (Bridges, Crutchfield, & Simpson, 1987) examined imprisonment rates for whites and nonwhites in thirty-nine Washington counties between 1980 and 1982. The authors concluded that increases in a county's minority ethnic makeup and urbanization were associated with heightened likelihoods of imprisonment for minorities but appeared to have no effect on the chances of incarceration for whites.

The work of Myers (1987), Myers and Talarico (1988), and Bridges and colleagues (1987) indicates the need for academics to consider characteristics of the area in which sentencing takes place. Their work demonstrated that sentencing can be affected by forces outside of the individual case at hand. In doing so, they expanded the methodological battlefield.

JUDICIAL RACE

Changes in societal attitudes and laws have increased the numbers of minorities attending law schools and receiving appointments as jurists. At a time when black justices were almost nonexistent, researchers had assumed that disparities in sentences resulted from racism by white judges against black defendants. Recent increases in the number of black justices gave rise to studies that consider both the defendant's and judge's ethnicity. Cassia Spohn (1990), for example, considered whether white judges are more likely than black judges to discriminate against black defendants. To explore this possibility, Spohn collected information on 4,710 felony cases processed in Detroit between 1976 and 1978.[29]

Spohn (1990) concluded that legal matters, such as the offenses for which defendants were convicted or their prior criminal records, "clearly overshadowed" the effects of any other items with respect to sentencing (1990, p. 1206). Overall, the race of judges and defendants played a minimal, if any, role in sentencing. There were, however, some circumstances in which judicial race may have affected penalties. Black judges were slightly less likely than white judges to send offenders to jail. This judicial leniency, however, did not favor black defendants. Black defendants were sentenced more harshly than whites by both black and white judges.[30]

BIAS IN ALTERNATIVE SENTENCING

Most studies of sentencing have focused on felony courts where increased use of punishment guidelines have attempted to limit judicial discretion. James Meeker and colleagues (Meeker, Jesilow, & Aranda, 1992) took a different tactic. They collected data on 106 first-time nonserious misdemeanants sentenced to community service work after pleading guilty in a southern California municipal court district. The municipal court judges were free to exercise their discretion and determine the length of sentences as well as where sentences were to be served.

The strategy employed by the researchers also allowed them to avoid some methodological problems. For example, because the defendants were all first-time offenders, measurement of prior criminal record was not a concern. Further, the study was not limited to the sentencing of offenders guilty of a limited list of crimes. Rather, defendants had committed an extensive variety of crimes, yet there was little variation between the seriousness of the offenses since they were all misdemeanors. In addition, all the offenders had entered pleas of guilty, so there was no need to consider the effects of trials or other items associated with the courtroom work group and sentencing.

Meeker and his colleagues (1992, p. 200) concluded from their limited sample that the duration of offenders' community service was determined by the seriousness of their offenses, but that their placements might be affected by other matters. In particular, Hispanics and males were more likely to be ordered by judges to pick up trash and do other tasks along California's freeways, a placement the justices felt was very unpleasant. Whites and women did their community service in more pleasant surroundings. The authors (1992, p. 200) suggested that the placement bias was due to the unrestricted ability of the judges to assign offenders as they saw fit; discretion led to bias.

SUMMARY OF BIAS LITERATURE IN JUDICIAL SENTENCING

It is readily apparent from our review of the relevant studies that the seriousness of offenders crimes combined with their prior criminal records most influences the severity of punishments judges impose on them. These two factors, in fact, consistently explain most of the variability in sentence severity (Chiricos & Bales, 1991; Gordon & Glaser, 1991; Gottfredson, 1978/1981; Green, 1961; Myers, 1987; Petersilia & Turner, 1985; Spohn, 1990; Uhlman, 1977; 1979; Zatz, 1984).

Extralegal matters appear to have minimal effects on judicially ordered penalties. While early researchers (before 1950) often found evidence of racial bias, they seldom considered the impact of the important legal items (i.e., seriousness of offense and prior record) on their results. In response to criticisms raised during the 1970s, researchers utilized sophisticated methods and statistics to study judicial sentencing. These examinations, for the most part, reported limited effects of extralegal offender characteristics on judicial punishments (Bridges et al., 1987; Eisenstein & Jacob, 1977; Lizotte, 1978; Meeker et al., 1992; Myers, 1987; Myers & Talarico, 1988; Petersilia & Turner, 1985; Spohn, 1990; Uhlman, 1977; 1979; Welch et al., 1984; Zatz, 1984).

The evidence assures us that judges are fairly color blind when sentencing defendants. Legally relevant criteria are much more important. But the evidence also suggests that sentencing is a complex decision that is not limited simply to an offense, an offender, a possible victim, and a judge, prosecutor, and possible defense attorney. Sentencing may reflect many external factors including the social mores of the surrounding communities (from which the judges are often drawn), the strength of pressures on key personnel in the justice system, and the amount of unrest between racial or other groups in the district. Studies that utilize official government data may never disentangle all the important items.

To learn something new about judicial sentencing we decided to take a step back from the methodological fray and to plan a study that would explore judicial sentencing employing data that we would collect. We chose to interview judges and compile sentencing information in their courtrooms. In this manner, we gained some control over the selection and integrity of the information. The following chapter focuses on the judges' answers to our questions and discusses the manners in which bias may enter their decisions.

CHAPTER 3

"DOING JUSTICE":
THE FORMATION OF
JUDICIAL BIAS IN SENTENCING

Judges we interviewed perceived their role in the courts as "doing justice" and judicial discretion, they argued, was necessary if they were to fulfill this function. As a result, they attempted to expand their use of mechanisms that grant them greater preferences. Such techniques include refusal of guilty pleas and assignment of offenders to probation and community service. The judges often expressed resentment for circumstances, such as mandatory sentencing and overcrowded jails, that limited their autonomy with respect to punishment. As judges, they believed they were in the best position to make sentencing decisions.

The judges' stated attempts to "do justice," however, also suggest the manner in which bias may creep into judicial decisions. Their formulations often included extralegal factors, such as defendants' attitudes or motivations for committing their offenses. Of equal importance in the creation of bias in judicial sentencing were the judges' views on the purpose of punishment. Defendants with similar records facing comparable charges might receive varied punishments from the judges because the sentencing philosophies of the justices differed.

Our findings may not be applicable to all judges. We interviewed twenty-seven municipal justices[1] who sat in a metropolitan county in southern California. The county has similarities to other urban areas: a diverse ethnic population living in a high-density urban center surrounded by comparatively affluent zones that are predominantly populated by whites.

The county differs from other areas in that it has a high per capita income and is considered by many to be politically conservative. These items may affect the overall portrait of the judges who are elected by county judicial district or appointed by the governor. Even the appointed judges, however, must run for reelection. It is reasonable to assume, on the one hand, that the judges are reflective of local sentiment because they must gather the population's support to win enough votes to secure and retain their judgeships. Judges who never stand for election, on the other hand, may vary in their levels of agreement with the attitudes of those in their communities because they normally were chosen by agents outside of the neighborhoods in which the judges serve.

The affluence of many county residents may also affect the general crime picture and, concomitantly, the types of cases the judges moderate. Experts familiar with the area agree that it has far more than its share of white-collar crimes, but few of these cases are handled by the municipal court judges who are the focus of this research.

In one important aspect, however, these justices do not stand out as remarkably different from other metropolitan municipal magistrates. They are busy: together, they disposed of an average of over twelve thousand criminal cases per judge in 1991 (Judicial Council of California, 1992, pp. 78–81).

We tried to contact more than forty judges. Two of the judges on our list had recently retired and we were unable to contact them. Three judges told us they were unwilling to participate in the study, and we were also unable to arrange interviews with seventeen justices although they said they wished to talk to us and we continued in our efforts to arrange interviews with them during a fifteen-month span.

THE JUDGES

We interviewed twenty-seven judges.[2] All the conferences were scheduled at the judges' convenience and all but two of the meetings took place in their chambers. One judge was interviewed in the courtroom due to a recent injury that greatly affected the justice's mobility, and one chose to be interviewed in a courtroom with staff present as witnesses. All but one interview was tape-recorded, always with the judges' permission.

Demographically, the interviewed judges do not differ much from those discussed elsewhere (e.g., see Emmert & Glick, 1987; Feeley, 1979; Flango & Ducat, 1979; Glick & Emmert, 1986; Goldman, 1985; Myers & Talarico, 1987; Vines, 1962). All the judges had been practicing attorneys prior to their appointments. They tended to be white males who were educated in California, although a substantial number (8 of 27) were women—evidence of the increasing numbers of females gaining admittance to state bars (Berkson, 1982). Most of the judges in our sample (22 of 27) were appointed by the governor and had to run for re-election after their initial terms were completed.

During a forty-five minute interview, the judges were asked a variety of questions regarding their careers and the day-to-day concerns of their courtrooms. We wanted to learn how they felt about judicial discretion and their perceptions of their role in the criminal justice system, as well as their thoughts on different punishment mechanisms, such as fines, jail, and community service.[3] We supplemented the information judges gave us with interviews of court administrators, assistant district attorneys, public defenders, court executive officers, and other individuals who provided background information about the courts and their positions.

"Doing Justice": The Judges Talk about Their Roles

Generally, the municipal court judges felt their role in the system was to achieve justice. "Doing justice," as the judges often referred to it, involves protecting those convicted of minor offenses from an overzealous and overloaded system, while simultaneously meting out punishments designed to prevent reoccurrences of criminal activities.

Nearly all of the judges (25 of 27) felt their roles entailed guaranteeing that people were treated fairly and ensuring that justice was carried out for both offenders and the rest of society. This role, as they stated, involves remaining neutral at all times, protecting naive defendants from a system that may be foreign and difficult to understand, and administering justice in a fair manner. Defendants processed through the criminal justice system should "feel they have been treated with respect" and should feel that the judge considered their accounts of the alleged crimes.

According to the judges, punishments, too, should be fair. "Just" sentences should be tailored to offenders and should take into consideration information about individuals' backgrounds (especially the presence or absence of prior criminal activities) and their abilities to comply with sentences or pay fines. The justices felt that their role required them to balance offenders' rights to fairness and society's rights to be protected. One judge told us:

> You assess the case and the person in front of you and try to determine what society's interest in that person is and balance it against your limited resources and your ability to influence some form of positive outcomes for both the defendant and the people who would be affected by any future actions he makes.

The judicial balancing act was handled differently by the various judges. One magistrate, for example, felt that "doing justice" included making sure that punishment deals offered to defendants were attractive enough to induce them to plead guilty, but not so attractive that defendants escaped appropriate punishment. This judge explained that his case load often exceeded 100 cases daily and, in order to dispose of cases, he "spends a minute" with the case and makes the defendant an offer. At that stage, the judge has a:

> duty to have enough sensitivity to get what needs to be gotten from the defendant in the case but to make it attractive enough so that he doesn't want to take a risk and go to trial. . . . I have the role of handling the calendar in such a manner that most of those cases are disposed of

but that it is done such that everybody has a sense that justice was done. The defendant, the police, the public, everybody feels that we didn't give the case away.

A very small minority of the judges (2 of 27) felt their role was to enforce the law. These judges, both of whom had been private attorneys before coming to the bench, felt that deterring individual offenders from future crimes would protect society from continued victimization. Through enforcing the law, they aspired to pressure offenders out of criminal activity.

Barriers to "Doing Justice":
Limits on the Judges' Autonomy

As a group, the judges valued their discretion and spoke poorly of factors that limited their freedom to sentence as they felt necessary. They believed they were in the best position to make sentencing decisions. Without discretion, they argued, they could not tailor sentences to individual offenders and "do justice." Mandatory sentences and jail overcrowding were but two of the factors that limited the judges' discretion.

Although not all judges told us they took jail capacities into consideration, many did. They realized that sentencing offenders to jail did not necessarily mean they would be so punished because the sheriff often released inmates to ameliorate overcrowding. The judges were frustrated by their inability to determine how long violators would spend incarcerated. One judge noted, "even accounting for good time and work time, we have no control over what the sheriff is going to do with somebody." Faced with increasing numbers of offenders and no room to house new prisoners, the judges were forced to rely on alternative sentences, such as community service or house arrest.

The judges also disliked the mandatory sentences that served as "shackles" limiting their discretion. Mandatory sentences are set by legislatures to ensure that offenders will receive a certain penalty if they are convicted. They limit judicial discretion both by setting specific sentences and also by limiting which penalty options a judge may employ.

None of the judges felt that there should be more mandatory sentences at the municipal court level. All had at least one negative comment about them. Illustrative are the reflections of one judge:

> To me, I think it [mandatory sentencing] is unfortunate. I think if you look at a thousand cases and sentence everyone the same . . . there's going to be some injustice because every case is different. People don't always do things for the same motivation. One person is different from the next. One person is not dangerous as opposed to somebody else and there might be reasons to give somebody a break. But you can't give them the break.

Overall, the judges felt that mandatory sentences erode their essential discretion (11 of 27), don't work (9 of 27), are too harsh (5 of 27), remove their ability to tailor sentences to offenders (3 of 27), and make their lives more difficult (1 of 27).[4]

One specific mandatory penalty that appeared to offend the judges was the ninety-day jail sentence for being under the influence of a controlled substance (California Health and Safety Code 11550). The judges questioned the fairness of punishing these offenders with lengthy jail terms when it appears that jail does very little to help offenders deal with their addictions.[5] The judges also felt that the penalties were unfair because they targeted individuals who may not be causing harm to others in society. The following judge, for example, felt that drunk drivers pose a much greater threat:

> Minimum sentences scare me. The one that really bothers me is the minimum sentence for Health and Safety Code section 11550. It's ninety days in jail. Yet, the minimum sentence for drunk driving, where you're driving a four thousand pound weapon in danger of killing people is zero days in jail. . . . [Drunk drivers] are much more dangerous to society . . . than somebody just being under the influence of a controlled substance.

A small number of the judges (5 of 27) supported the mandatory sentences implemented for driving under the influence

(DUI). They were willing to relinquish their discretion in order to inform the public (and their fellow brethren) that drinking and driving is no longer acceptable by the rest of society and to ensure that the public knows the penalty. One judge, for example, explained that while he is "sorry mandatory sentencing happened," he feels mandatory DUI penalties are necessary to protect society from drunk drivers and establish appropriate sentencing parameters for judges. He told us, "There's a minimum sentence of 120 days in jail on the third time for driving under the influence . . . I can promise you we couldn't get all the judges in the state to agree with that sentence. I mean, they just wouldn't do it."

Mandatory fines also met with the judges' disapproval. They hypothesized that they had been enacted by the legislature for the wrong reasons. These judges resented the fact that their courtrooms were one of the state's financial resources and pressure was put on them to use fines where they did not feel fines were just. The judges felt no particular animosity toward the defendants in their courtrooms and saw no reason to penalize them for the state's financial woes. The following judge, for example, explained:

> You have a lot of people coming into our court. Times are so hard, things are so expensive, that you get people coming in here for parking tickets . . . dressed very nicely, to save five dollars on a parking ticket. That's how life is nowadays. You get a lot of people coming in here who aren't John Dillinger, coming in on their first moving violation. Those people deserve to be treated like the good people that they are, to be given breaks. I don't personally feel that I'm under any obligation whatsoever to balance the budget on the backs of people like that coming into court. And I won't do it.

Some of the judges felt that mandatory sentences made them into automatons. Since mandatory penalties erode judicial discretion, judges could become unnecessary expenses. The judges resented the impression that they may be figureheads with little or no power to do justice. The following judge contended:

> I don't think you ever want to take the discretionary call away from the courts. I think it's a very dangerous thing to do. . . . Once you start doing mandatory minimum sentences, politics gets involved rather than justice and fairness in my opinion. If you want to have mandatory sentences in everything, why do you need a judge? Just have a computer up there and when the guy is found guilty, just punch the computer and it will pop up the sentence for you.

Some justices recognized that the combination of overcrowded jails and mandatory sentences occasioned the transfer of discretion from judges to the sheriff:

> It is now routine in this county that if you give someone thirty days in the [county] jail, the sheriff will instead order weekends on a work program that he sets up. For example, the sheriff can kick the person out on weekends if he wants to, therefore making the mandatory sentence meaningless.

One judge lamented that offenders who commit more serious offenses and are given jail time "actually get lighter penalties" than those who commit less serious offenses. The reason for this, he told us, was that offenders who are sentenced to, say, five days of community service must complete all five days, while those sent to jail may, depending on the sheriff's needs, "end up doing two or three days of community service."

"Removing the Shackles": The Judges' Techniques for Expanding Discretion

The judges' dislike of limiting forces such as mandatory sentences and overcrowded jails caused the magistrates to devise methods to bypass them and restore at least part of their discretion to "do justice." They told us they used a variety of methods to expand their discretion, including refusing plea bargains, assignment of offenders to probation and community service, creative interpretation of statutes, and recommendations to the probation department to allow alternative placements for mandatory sentences.

Refusing to accept plea bargains, the judges argued, allowed them to "do justice." For example, when the sentences agreed on by the district attorney and defense counsel appeared to be either too harsh or too lenient, the judges said they rejected the bargains. Very few cases in the lower courts, however, involve defense counsel, and, if cases that do involve them receive special treatment, a subtle bias may be at work.

The judges also told us they utilized creative interpretations of laws to expand their discretion. Whenever statute wording allowed them to escape imposing mandatory sentences on offenders they felt deserved less, the judges used alternative sanctions. Some statutes (littering laws, for example) specifically mention that mandatory sentences may be suspended where "justice would best be served by suspension of that order," thus opening the door to creative interpretation by judges. The following justice explained this tactic in further detail:

> There is an interplay between the legislature and the courts. If the statute is ambiguous at all, the judges will try to use that to avoid the mandatory language when they feel it's appropriate. When the legislature hears that they'll go back and revise the language to try to make it more mandatory. So it's an interplay between the two branches on that.

Related to creative interpretation of statute wording was the judges' ability to dismiss charges against defendants if the justices feel it is "in the interests of justice."[6] One judge, for example, told us he dismisses fines for handicapped parking violations if the offender had a documented medical emergency. Each dismissal, however, requires a written justification by the judge, a task that the justices may find difficult to substantiate under some circumstances. Judges' personal assessments that offenders are unlikely to commit future crimes, for example, may be difficult to put in words that satisfy the legal requirement of the statute.

The judges said they also expanded their discretion by making recommendations to the probation department regarding punishments. When mandatory sentences seemed unjust, the justices imposed mandatory jail sentences and then lobbied the probation department to approve alternative placements. If the probation department agreed, the offender would not serve the mandatory term in jail. This method was utilized most often to allow offenders to spend time in private residential drug and alcohol programs instead of the county jail. Although such a system favored offenders with the ability to pay for such programs, the judges felt it helped alleviate overcrowding in the jails in addition to getting offenders into the treatment programs they needed.

Assignment of defendants to probation was an often-mentioned mechanism by which judges expanded their discretion, and avoided imposing jail sentences on those they felt did not deserve incarceration. Probation, within the judges framework of "doing justice," gave offenders the opportunity to "clean up their lives." Some of the judges attempted to give the violators an assist with their rehabilitations by ordering them to attend treatment sessions as part of their conditional releases.

Probation, according to the judges, might also be wielded to "leverage" defendants into long sentences. One judge in particular operated what she called her "bank." She would suspend offenders' short jail terms and assign them to probation. She designated these suspended sentences "time in the bank." She would then simply wait until they committed new crimes and "accumulated probations" and owed her "inordinate amounts of jail time." When she felt they owed her "enough time to make an impression on their lives," she would "max them out consecutively." By revoking their probations and reinstating the original penalties, this judge was able to sentence several offenders to lengthy jail terms (she told us she had people serving two- and three-year spans). This strategy, she argued, allowed her to achieve justice. First-time offenders, on the one hand, could be released on probation, certainly one of the more lenient sentencing options available to the judge. If offenders did not repeat their crimes, they continued their lives uninterrupted by the justice system. Repeat violators, on the other hand, might be leveraged into lengthy incarcerations. The types of offenders this judge manipulated into long sentences included, for the most part, chronic drunks and drug addicts. This judge firmly believed she was acting in the best interests of the individuals. She told us about several offenders she had sentenced to long jail terms and expressed concern for their well-being, a concern that she felt required forcing a change in self-destructive behavior:

> I just want him [an alcoholic she maxed out for two and a half years for repeated convictions of being drunk in public] to stay alive. . . . I've had three or four people die on me who have either been run over in the street or frozen to death because they drink and the blood alcohol kills them.[7]

"FILLING THE VOID":
JUDGES' VIEWS OF COMMUNITY SERVICE

The judges often told us that they ordered defendants to complete community service in lieu of other penalties, and these exchanges were a method by which the justices expanded their discretion. They overwhelmingly supported the punishment option under at least some circumstances. Only one judge disapproved wholly of the sanction (she felt that offenders would not comply with the orders, thus necessitating sending them to jail).

Some judges posited that community service offered an equality of punishment that was not possible with fines. They viewed it as a way to bridge across socioeconomic classes and equalize penalties. If the rich and poor alike perform the same types of duties, there may be less inequity brought about because some offenders have money with which to pay fines and others do not. One judge, for example, told us, "It's a more egalitarian situation. A person [with money] has to go out and pick up trash along the freeway as does a poor person. . . . That's probably the ideal situation."

The use of community service, however, also introduced a subtle bias into punishments. Recognition that offenders without a steady income cannot pay fines motivated most of the judges' remarks about this sentencing alternative. They converted fines into community service to allow those who could not afford payments to work off their penalties; indigents fulfilled service orders while the financially capable paid fees. One judge, for example, told us:

> Take a drunk driving offense, for instance. It's $390.00 plus penalty assessment [a legislated fee paid in addition to the fine]. That comes to $1180.00 for the first offense; that is very hard to pay. Are you just going to throw that guy in jail and let the rich man walk? So, we do a substantial amount of community service for drunk driving for indigent people. Basically, they do thirteen days of community service in lieu of the fine. Petty theft is . . . poor people . . . [who] wouldn't have been stealing if they could afford [a] fine. So, we just give them five days of community service.

By employing community service sentences, the judges avoided the dilemma of fining people who could not afford the penalties. But equity was not achieved when they allowed the financially able to pay for their crimes.[8]

Unlike the consensus regarding community service in lieu of fines, using public service to replace a jail term was quite controversial among the judges. While some of the judges saw community service as a way to lessen jail overcrowding, they did not feel that this was its proper purpose.

> I think that community service sentencing has a valid place, in relation to particular types of offenses. It's a good idea. The unfortunate aspect . . . is that we get in situations where . . . a more appropriate penalty might be some custody time. But, through a lack of funding and lack of jail space, we don't have the jails to use for those particular offenders. If in place of that, we give someone community service, I don't think that's a very good situation. . . . [W]e have a number of people who think that community service doesn't answer the bill.

The judges, on the one hand, were frustrated by early release dates caused by jail overcrowding. They knew that some offenders would not serve any time at all on a jail sentence. A community service sentence, on the other hand, represented a punishment the judge knew offenders would have to complete. Public service represented a second choice for these judges because, although not as appropriate for their goals as jail, it was preferable to the remaining options (for the most part, probation or fines).

Community service fit neatly within the concept of "doing justice," through its often unique fairness-oriented nature. Offenders could "right their wrongs" by working to improve the quality of life of society in general. Which assignment they made, according to the judges, was based on the appropriateness of the site for the offender. Judges, for example, told us they often sentenced those convicted of painting graffiti to "undo" the graffiti of others. These judges felt that working in certain placements may help the offender "see the error of his ways," and have a rehabilitative effect.

Specifying where offenders had to complete their hours gave the judges control over the distastefulness of the punishment, while still allowing them to tailor sentences to offenders. The justices viewed roadwork as a particularly unsavory assignment and tended to reserve it for offenders who may have merited jail time. As one judge noted:

> [Roadwork], I think, is a step between jail and community service because it's not jail, nor is it fun to do. People pick up litter on the freeways on weekends and they make them do that for eight hours and it's kind of hard.

Although the judges supported community service sentences in general, they saw a number of problems associated with implementing them. One such difficulty was the lack of supervision afforded at some of the placement sites. When offenders were not adequately supervised, they sometimes did not complete their assignments, and according to the judges, justice was not served; the offenders were not punished and society did not benefit from their service. As noted by the following judge:

If you send someone out to pick trash in the parks that's
great. The parks are clean and it serves the public and
the person's out there doing it. But, if they're sent out
there and supervision lacks and they sit under some tree
and have a cold drink or a beer while they are on that
thing and they're not supervised, it becomes a joke and
that reflects back on the court.

Community service sentences returned to the judges a sense of
fair and certain punishment. When they were unable to
enforce jail penalties due to overcrowding, community service could be implemented. Community service, according to
the judges, allowed them to control penalties and to fit punishments to offenders. As one judge noted, community service "fills the void" when traditional fine or jail options are
not appropriate for particular defendants.

PREVENTING FUTURE CRIME:
THE JUDGES' PUNISHMENT PHILOSOPHIES

There are four generally recognized punishment philosophies: rehabilitation, retribution, deterrence, and incapacitation. Rehabilitation is an effort to end criminal behavior by
changing the individual. Punishment, according to advocates
of rehabilitation, should involve treatment designed to "cure"
offenders of their criminality.

Punishment based on retribution attempts to restore balance to society, while establishing proper parameters of behavior. According to retributive theory, we punish offenders to
take away any advantages they might have gained from their
illegal acts, thus restoring the balance society seeks and satis-
fying our desire for revenge (the offender has hurt someone, so
we will hurt the offender). In addition, the use of harsh punishments for wrongdoing places the misbehavior outside the
boundaries of what "good" people do and defines the conduct
as intolerable.

Deterrence is the belief that criminals are rational individuals who weigh the costs and benefits of illegal acts and

decide that the benefits of crime outweigh the costs. Offenders are punished, then, to maintain the perception that crime has high costs, thus thwarting the commission of illegal acts.

Finally, incapacitation is the belief that a majority of crimes are committed by relatively few individuals. When these offenders are behind bars, they cannot victimize society. If these few offenders are selectively incarcerated, the argument goes, crime rates will go down.

Only four of the twenty-seven judges stated that they follow a single sentencing philosophy. The majority varied from situation to situation. The judges tailor sentencing philosophies to individual offenders based on the judges' opinions on how to best prevent future crimes.

According to the judges, their primary goal when sentencing was preventing recurrence of criminal activities. Theoretically, all four major punishment philosophies work toward this purpose. Rehabilitated offenders will not participate in future crimes once their special needs have been met. Incapacitated offenders cannot commit offenses against the public while in jail. Deterred potential offenders comply with laws and offenders who have been punished may obey laws to avoid further punishment in the future. Finally, retributive punishments remind society's members of what is expected of them, and nudges them toward conformity.

Deterrence was the most popular philosophy among the judges. Two-thirds (18 of 27) of the judges stated that deterrence was one of the purposes they had in mind when deciding sentences. The justices were not particularly interested in general deterrence—punishing criminals as a warning to potential violators. Rather, punishment was aimed at discouraging future violations by those they sentenced. One of the judges, for example, felt that penalties handed out in misdemeanor courts cannot be considered as general deterrents to crime. Due to the low level of attention paid to the misdemeanor courts, both by the media and the public, sentences crafted by lower court judges do not "deter other people, except those in the courtroom." Because of this belief, the judge felt that his primary goal was to individualize sentences so that he could deter specific offenders while simultaneously meting out fair punishments.

Since the greater society may not be deterred by their sentences, there may be more of a judicial culture in the misdemeanor courts favoring personalized justice. According to the judges, individual characteristics of offenders are important when fashioning deterrence-oriented sentences. Offenders are assessed as to the likelihoods that they will repeat their crimes. Those individuals who the judges feel will not commit new illegalities receive lenient penalties. For those that the judges feel may commit new offenses, sentences must be enough to deter, but not too harsh, lest justice suffer. Judges considered many things when deciding appropriate penalties, including offender characteristics. Young violators, for example, were punished severely by one judge, because he felt he could deter them with harsh sentences, while older offenders, he posited, were unlikely to learn the intended lesson.

The second most mentioned sentencing philosophy was rehabilitation (14 of 27).[9] The judges who adopted this ideology felt that offenders needed to be helped with their problems. Each of these judges had numerous "success stories" of offenders who had gone through treatment and were now "cured." One judge's desk even sported a smiling picture of a former defendant who had reformed his ways after completing an alcohol treatment program.

In place of traditional jail sentences, the interviewed judges who employed the rehabilitative model said they preferred to send offenders with mental health problems to counseling programs that addressed specific needs (for example, drug abuse, anger management, and alcohol abuse). The judges felt that jail sentences seldom assisted those suffering from depression and other psychological maladies with reintegration into society, which they viewed as a way to prevent repeat offenses.

The judges were not eternal optimists whose vision was blurred by their idealistic hopes. They realized that all defendants cannot be rehabilitated. Many judges told about offenders who they unsuccessfully tried to assist. The justices also understood that all individuals do not welcome treatment. Offenders generally view interruptions of their lives in negative terms and sometimes feel that they do not need to participate in care programs. The judges coerced some violators into treatment with threats of severe sanctions. They would suspend the harsh sentences if offenders completed programs.

A few judges questioned the role of rehabilitation programs in the criminal justice system. They felt the courts do not have the social work ethic necessary to rehabilitate offenders. One judge decried the rehabilitation system as a fortune-telling exercise gone awry.

Retribution was the third most mentioned sentencing philosophy (10 of 27). The judges indicated that retribution entered into their decisions, resulting in particularly stern sentences, when offenders repeatedly victimized vulnerable individuals:

> This asshole has beaten up fifteen different girlfriends and . . . you know the son-of-a-bitch is going to beat up his next girlfriend. If deterrence were the only reason to sentence, you'd say "Geez, I just can't deter you, Mr. Jones. I know you're going to do it again, so I might as well not give you any time in jail." So, therefore, if you're at all intellectually honest, the only reason you're punishing someone is just because it feels good to punish him and also the last person he hurt knows he's doing six months or a year in jail or whatever.

Only one-fourth of the judges said they sentenced based on incapacitation theory (7 of 27). Incapacitation-oriented sentences, according to the judges, are implemented when society needs to be protected from the offender's crimes. Unlike other punishments, incapacitation always involves long jail terms. By repeating their crimes, offenders demonstrate that they have not been deterred or rehabilitated by earlier attempts to curb their criminality. An interviewed judge explained, "For the guys that keep coming back, you just warehouse them for as long as you can."

The Factors Considered by the Judges in Sentencing

To determine which punishment philosophy should be implemented for each defendant, the judges weight certain factors in each case and use those factors to assist them in deciding sentences. Such items as prior convictions and characteristics of the offense and offender are items considered by judges when imposing sentences.

According to the justices, one of the most important individual factors to consider is prior criminal history. A previous record indicates an offender's potential for reform as well as the individual's internalization of a criminal lifestyle (which reflects the likelihood of deterring the offender from future illegal acts). Two-thirds of the judges (18 of 27) cited evidence of a prior record as a factor that would result in a harsher sentence. These judges felt that, unlike first-time offenders, chronic criminals had to be dealt with harshly in order to prevent them from causing future harms.

The seriousness of defendants' crimes also related to the severity of their sentences. More than half (14 of 27) of the judges said they consider the nature and type of offense when fashioning punishments. Generally, the more serious an offense, the harsher the resulting sanction. The following judge told how severity of the crime can increase the harshness of sentences for first-time offenders, a class of individuals usually treated leniently:

> [The sentence] depends on the situation. If you have a first-time offender on a petty theft or some such thing like that, you don't usually get too excited about it. When you start having people who are using guns and holding up people or something that is more of a violent nature, you are most concerned.

The judges also considered the presence of aggravating or mitigating circumstances. Over half of the judges (14 of 27) stated that they consider such things as the vulnerability of the victim, the presence of violence, the offender's level of sophistication (e.g., if the offense was well-planned), the amount of damage or injury, or the presence of mitigating factors when deciding sentences. The effect of mitigating factors on sentences may introduce bias as they include subjective items, such as stress in the offender's home, recent unemployment, or other traumas in the defendant's life. The following judge told how considering mitigating factors could result in a lenient sentence:

> For instance, a petty theft can be as simple as taking a six ounce steak from a meat store. . . . If you see that [the thief] has family, that he lost a job three weeks ago, that he has children, that he can't get on SSI or some other such state-mandated program to provide the necessities for relief for that interim period of time, then you have to assume, just taking those things into consideration, that this is not a real "criminal" person. This individual, more likely than not, did this deed for the purpose of food for his family . . . he will obviously get considerably more benefit of the court's feeling for the lesser gravity of that crime than the individual who has had some drug contacts before.

Almost half of the judges (12 of 27) said they consider the violator's background when sentencing. This catchall variable considers such things as the offender's family situation, age, and other social variables. The judges felt that these social variables indicated the offender's need for special programs or leniency. Recently ill individuals, for example, may not be as "criminal" as other offenders.

A fourth of the judges (7 of 27) mentioned that the offender's potential for rehabilitation is a factor they consider when imposing sentences. This component is based on the judge's assessment of the individual and includes many of the previously mentioned factors: the person's background, prior record, and type of offense. According to the judges, these factors, taken together, indicate whether an individual will benefit from treatment.

A minority of judges (4 of 27) said that the suggestions of the attorneys (the district attorney's office and defense counsel) are factors to be considered when determining penalties. When hearing plea bargains, judges know very little about the cases before them. The respective attorneys are much more likely to have specific details and know the "worth" of a case.

The judge may then rely on the attorneys to make suggestions. Even judges who accept suggestions from attorneys, however, point out that the sentence must seem fair for both sides.

Approximately 10 percent of the judges (3 of 27) said they consider the offender's attitude when imposing punishments. When the judges feel offenders are remorseful or feel sorry for what they have done, the justices are more likely to sentence less harshly. The reverse, however, is also true. Those offenders the judges perceive as "defiant," "confrontational," or "belligerent" may find themselves with stricter penalties than their less obnoxious counterparts. This attitude dimension may represent a source of bias in the system. Those offenders perceived as rebellious, which may well be culturally determined, may be sentenced harshly irrespective of other more important factors.

Other items mentioned by the judges as useful during sentencing included public sentiment toward a crime, the offender's ability to pay a fine, restitution to any victims, the offender's behavior between the time of arrest and his trial, and overcrowding at the jail. These factors were considered to be of secondary importance in the ultimate sentencing decision.

HOW THE JUDGES ACHIEVED CONSISTENCY AMONG THEIR SENTENCES

Judges told us they have methods for achieving consistency in a system that relies heavily on individualization of sentences. As a group, the interviewed justices valued agreement in their sentencing. One judge explained:

> I think the judges want to be consistent with what other judges are doing regarding sentencing. I don't think we want to be so far afield where you walk in one door and the sentence may be "X" and if you go to a different judge, it may be just totally different. They try to keep it somewhat consistent with the other judges.

In general, the judges did not want penalties for similar crimes to vary too much because offenders may feel they were harshly punished, not because of their own acts, but because they got a "hanging judge" who sentences everyone severely. The judges stressed that offenders should feel they were treated fairly, that they deserved whatever punishments were imposed.

There are several ways that judges attempt to achieve sentencing uniformity without violating the canons of judicial conduct that prohibit them from considering information gained from communications that take place outside of court (California Judges Association, 1987/1990). The interviewed justices interpreted this canon to mean that they must not discuss their cases with others lest they become biased by the information received during the ensuing discussions. To illustrate the tenacity with which the judges held this belief, one judge replied, "Actually it's illegal to do that," when asked how she achieved consistency with her colleagues. Of course, it was not illegal to impose sentences similar to those imposed by her colleagues; the illegality involved allowing people outside the courtroom to establish penalties.

One way judges achieve consistency with their colleagues' sentences is through information sharing at meetings with other justices. During these formal and informal meetings, judges do not discuss individual cases per se, so much as they discuss types of cases.

The judges also get information from the attorneys working on the cases. One judge told us that agreement is accomplished because "we are all working with the same attorneys," who travel from courtroom to courtroom and the judges can depend on them to some degree. This cooperation is consistent with Nardulli's (1978) and Eisenstein and Jacobs's (1977) concept of the "courtroom elite" who work together to process cases.

Judges can also glean sentencing information from probation reports. As offenders are processed for probation violations, judges hearing the cases are able to see how the original judge sentenced the offender. The following judge explained this process:

We write our offers on the file, what we believe the case is worth; and other judges are not committed to that at all, but at least it gives you an idea of what someone else is thinking of the case and the value of the case.

One judge told us that he carries a "ball park" sentencing sheet with him to the bench. As he explained, this sheet served to remind him how he had sentenced in the past and helped him avoid large discrepancies.

Some of the judges indicated that consistency was not as important to them as doing what seemed just. While these judges did not feel that agreement was evil, they felt that judges should not attempt to be congruous with their colleagues. They felt, that above all else, judges should do what is right given the individual case. Such justices might be likely to deviate from their colleagues' sentencing and create feelings of inequity among defendants.

Conclusion and Discussion

According to the judges, their goal in the criminal justice system was to "do justice," which included justice for both offenders and society. Efforts to limit judicial discretion, they believed, sharply hinder judges' abilities to implement what they feel is fair. They told us they often used methods to expand their discretion and tailor punishments to each defendant. As such, individual characteristics are of prime importance to the judges when they set sentences.

The fear, of course, is that the personalized punishments will reflect the justices' individual biases and that sentences will not be equitable. Since each judge weights the various factors differently, disparate sentences may result. One judge may feel a given offender is in need of counseling, while another may assess the same offender as someone who must be sentenced harshly to deter him or her from future crimes. Or offenses may appear to be the same, but the offenders may be quite different. One shoplifter, for example, may steal to support a drug habit. Another may steal to feed his or her children. Fashioning sentences based on individual characteristics may mean that sentences are fit to offenders instead of offenses.

The judges mentioned several items associated with individuals that they employ in their sentencing decisions: age, because they believe longer sentences make more of an impact on youthful offenders; attitude, because they expect defendants to act in a culturally accepted fashion; economic status, because they believe penalties affect people differently.

The judges also mentioned situations that affected their sentencing and probably introduced some bias into their punishments. Most prominent was the presence of defense counsel as the judges, among other things, respected their knowledge of the worth of cases. Also of importance was the ability of those defendants with regular incomes to afford fines and treatment programs.

Our interviews with the municipal court judges indicated that they differ from each other in many important ways, including their sentencing philosophies, their perspectives on the usefulness of mandatory sentences, and their willingness to assign certain types of punishments. Despite the efforts of the majority of the judges to achieve sentencing homogeneity (mostly through informal meetings), it is unlikely that they reach such uniformity, given their diverse views. Conformity in punishments for offenders is probably further undermined by a few justices' stated dislike for going along with their colleagues. For them, doing justice meant fashioning sentences to fit the circumstances they felt were important.

The judges as a group did not appear to worry too much about sentencing disparity between courtrooms. The few who mentioned it fretted most about the specter of "hanging judges"—courts where severe sentences are the norm.

Many offenders probably would disagree with the magistrates' perceptions of doing justice. The general public might disagree even more. People's perceptions of justice are composed of many facets, but a basic tenet is that we all be treated equally. Punishment seems unfair when it differs from individual to individual. A system that is viewed as inconsistent is unlikely to be considered legitimate (Andenaes, 1975).

The public is willing to allow some inequities in our court system. The evidence that sentencing judges treat men more severely than women does not now raise much consternation (Daly, 1994; Meeker et al., 1992). But such sentiment may go the way of earlier ideas that saw unequal treatment of minorities as fair.

Bias, as reflected in our interviews with judges, does not involve active decisions against members of certain groups. Rather, bias is more subtle and introduced by judicial attitudes that favor middle-class values (e.g., verbal skills, work, and conservative clothes). Such attitudes are strongly entrenched in our society and it is unlikely that limits on judicial discretion, for example by the imposition of mandatory sentences, eliminates such favoritism. Instead, the source of such biases is transferred to prosecutors, who make decisions about who to charge and for what, and jailers, who often determine actual release dates by their power over matters such as "good time." Such an outcome seems less than satisfactory, and may actually increase bias, since the actions of these two criminal justice actors are less accountable to public scrutiny than are those of judges.

In the next chapter we report the method we used to study the variation in our judges' sentencing and how we linked it to characteristics of the judges and the offenders who appeared in their courts.

CHAPTER 4

THE PROCESS OF DOING JUSTICE: WHAT THE DEFENDANTS DID

This study was not intended to prove or disprove the existence of judicial bias. We began with the assumption that bias exists. Obviously, from what the judges told us, similar offenders may be sentenced differentially—some may be sentenced leniently, while others receive the full measure of the law. The purpose of the analyses presented in this manuscript is to illuminate the complex conditions under which bias may occur and the factors that give rise to it.

The data on which we base our observations were derived from sixteen hundred misdemeanor arraignment hearings. The information was collected by trained observers, fifteen in all, in the courtrooms of twelve justices who we had interviewed. In the remainder of this chapter we discuss our methodology, paying particular attention to the limitations and advantages of the data set.

THE JUDGES

During our interviews with them, we gained the judges' consent to allow observers to sit in their courtrooms and record information of interest to our study. Criminal courtrooms are open to the public, and observers can attend proceedings as spectators without judicial consent. The benefit of gaining access through the judges, however, was that cooperation from courtroom personnel to clarify information that was not heard or understood during the trial was easily obtained. Evidence of offenders' prior records, for example, was not always presented in court and was not available in the public record.

While all the observed judges allowed us to collect data, some volunteered to help us with the task. These particularly cooperative judges agreed to provide us with information about offenders' prior records and to answer questions posed by the courtroom observers. They also made their courts more accessible to our observers. Some, for example, allowed our staff to sit in the jury box to maximize their ability to see the interactions taking place during the hearings or turned on loudspeakers so that our project people could better hear the judge's remarks. Two of the judges went so far as to allow our observers to accompany them to their chambers to ask questions and observe the bargaining and dialogue between the courtroom players.

We had originally planned to collect courtroom data on all the county's judges, but eventually confined our study to the justices who held arraignment hearings during a seven-month time frame in 1993. The judges told us they rotated assignments every six months to decrease the impact of courtroom work groups on sentencing and to increase the variety of cases they heard. This minimized the number of judges handling arraignment cases during the data collection period. We also lost several justices when one jurisdiction refused to assist us in our observations and we felt it best to avoid this court so as to not jeopardize data collection in the remaining districts. This resulted in a sample size of twelve judges. One of the twelve judges arraigned only major traffic offenses while the other justices processed criminal misdemeanors.

The twelve judges were evenly divided between male and female; ten were white, one was Asian, and one was Hispanic. Ten had been appointed to the bench and two had been elected. Before becoming judges, eight were prosecutors, two were private attorneys, one worked for the public defenders office, and one served as a county counsel.

The Observed Hearings

We had hoped to collect data from all types of hearings in the municipal courts under study. During pilot-testing, however, difficulties became obvious. Several project members, observing cases in a court to which we had access, attempted to collect as much information as possible about the defendants, their cases, the courtroom work groups, and the hearings.[1] It was our plan to begin by recording information on a wide inventory of factors and to narrow the list as necessary.

Several difficulties diminished the extent of the information we collected. Time was our greatest enemy. One person could not handle the fast-paced arraignments, which averaged two minutes and involved much hurried interaction. Our list had to be shortened to allow accurate recording of the details.

We also found that our observers did not always agree. Items, such as the quality of the defendants' dress, the nature of communications between judges and defendants, and the quality of evidence presented in court, were interpreted differently by each observer. What one labeled as quality evidence, for example, another labeled as poor. We realized that we could not gather information on these matters with an adequate level of reliability and decided to drop them from our list.

Some of the material we wanted was inaccessible to our courtroom observers. We could not, for example, determine defendants' employment situations (a measure of socioeconomic status). Details on the number of continuances, dates of original hearings, and prior records were not always available to us. Ascertaining the types of hearings or who participated in them was also difficult due to the confusion that often characterized the courtrooms under study.

Collection of some information proved impossible because the courtroom staff, whose assistance we needed, were often unavailable. During the hearings, important informants, such as clerks and bailiffs, were busy performing their duties and could not be questioned by our observers. After the hearings, these courtroom actors could be asked only a few brief questions to avoid imposing a burden on their personal schedules. We also found that they did not always have the answers we sought.

Details that were difficult to get from courtroom staff, we had hoped to obtain from the public records. They, however, were undependable and of dubious quality. This is not surprising; others have noted that record keeping at the municipal court level is often irregular and inadequate (Ashman, 1975, p. 31).

Our first obstacle with obtaining data from the criminal records in the county were that they were not truly public. One needed to know case numbers (available from the courtroom staff) to get details on criminal cases and this identifying information was difficult, at best, to obtain. In addition, even with case file numbers, the records were not easily located by the staff. Each defendant's file was inserted into a manila folder, with the larger files held together by rubber bands. Piles of these folders dotted the record's office floor like stalagmites in underground caverns. On one occasion, a clerk accidentally bumped a four-foot high pile, sending case records across the floor. The staff quickly shuffled the folders into a new pile. The staff was obviously overwhelmed by the amount of work. The result for us was that information of interest could not be gleaned from the hodge-podge array of manila folders.

To deal with these obstacles, we limited the factors we recorded and the type of hearings we observed. We chose only to study arraignment hearings, which are most frequently defendants' first appearances before a magistrate on their current charges. It is at these hearings that defendants are informed of their rights and the charges against them. Pleas are entered by defendants or their counsel. People who plead guilty in the municipal courts of the county under study are usually sentenced immediately. Trial dates may be set for those who plead not guilty.

There are a number of positive things to be said for limiting a study of judicial sentencing to arraignment hearings. We could standardize the information we collected by focusing on arraignment hearings. We could control for the length of time a case had been in the system, since by California law arraignments must take place within forty-eight hours of arrest. We could also eliminate the need to measure the amount of defense-initiated delay, since arraignments are offenders' first step in the court system. Elimination of these matters meant that we lost some material, but we strengthened the integrity of the information we collected.

It may be that arraignments are the best place to conduct research on judicial sentencing in that such an approach can avoid some of the pitfalls associated with previous efforts to explore sentencing decisions. It is at this stage that judges may exercise the most discretion. The addition of legal counsel at later stages of the process, for example, may increase the likelihood that a plea bargain will be struck and judges will merely be asked to ratify the deals. There is no legal requirement that individuals be represented by counsel at their arraignments. Defendants who want court-appointed counsel generally make this request during this first hearing. Further, some defendants may not know about their rights to counsel until the judge apprises them of this at their arraignments. As a result, some offenders may plead guilty and be sentenced without legal representation.[2]

An additional advantage of studying judicial sentencing at the arraignment stage is that the effects of mandatory penalties or jury imposed sentences are minimized. Offenders convicted at trial may likely face mandatory penalties over which judges have little control, or offenders may be sentenced by juries, such as in capital cases. Defendants, however, who plead guilty at their arraignments are, for the most part, placing themselves under the discretion of judges, and so, it is here that we should expect to find judicial bias as it exists.

It is likely, however, that information from arraignments may be idiosyncratic. A study that relies on arraignment hearings disproportionately includes defendants who do not have legal counsel. Also, the sentences imposed at such hearings differ from those assessed at other stages in the trial process (Meeker & Pontell, 1985).[3] Sentences imposed at arraignments may be less likely to involve defendants facing long jail sentences since such individuals may be more likely to take their chances at trial (Brickey & Miller, 1975; Feeley, 1979; McCall, 1978). Indeed, we found that those in our study who were not confronted with the specter of incarceration for their crimes were significantly more likely to plead guilty; 86 percent of those who could only be fined or have their licenses suspended pled guilty compared to 72 percent of those who could be jailed for their offenses (phi = .06, p < .05).

THE CHARGES

The data were collected in the courtrooms of twelve judges in one southern California county. The sample size of sixteen hundred cases is sufficiently large when compared with those of many other studies. Malcolm Feeley (1979), for example, observed 1,648 misdemeanor cases, while Maureen Mileski (1971) gathered data on only 417 misdemeanants, although Marcia Lipetz included more than twelve thousand cases in her 1980 sample.

An extensive variety of charges were arraigned in the municipal courts under study. Because some defendants were indicted for more than one offense, 2,592 charges were heard during the 1,600 arraignments. A total of 135 separate offenses were identified ranging from commonly known offenses such as driving under the influence of alcohol and petty theft to less well known offenses such as going through refuse and fueling a boat while docking. Our sample of misdemeanor arraignments included violations of state penal codes, vehicle codes, health and safety codes, welfare and institutions codes, business and professions codes, fish and game codes, and local ordinances.

Only 15 percent of the total number of offenses involved the violent, property, and public order crimes that one normally associates with the misdemeanor tribunals. Most of the judges' time was instead filled with hearing driving (32%), court related (30%), and drug and alcohol (20%) violations. By far, the most common illegalities were vehicle-related (820, excluding driving under the influence). Sixty percent of such charges were for driving on a suspended license (n = 492). Also included were 125 minor traffic violations (e.g., speeding and illegal turns),[4] 69 charges of driving without a license, 27 seat belt violations, and 21 charges of reckless driving. Other less frequently occurring charges included automobile "fix-it" tickets,[5] driving without vehicle registration, driving without insurance, driving with an open container of alcohol in the vehicle, participating in a speed contest, driving on an invalid license, driving on a revoked license, possessing an altered driver's license, driving on a beach, and driving with expired registration tags.

The second most frequent category in our sample was court-related offenses. These charges stemmed from violations of court mandates. In all, 775 such charges appeared in our data. Nearly half (45%) of these were for failure to appear in court (n = 351). Another 30 percent (n = 237) of the charges were for not fulfilling fine obligations or completing programs to which the offenders had been assigned, drunk driving programs for the most part. Our sample also included defendants who appeared because they had failed to complete community service obligations (n = 69), violated their probations (n=94), failed to serve jail sentences (n = 7),[6] or violated court orders, such as failure to pay child support (n = 16).

The third most common offense category was drug- or alcohol-related charges. There were 522 such charges in our sample, of which 40 percent were for driving under the influence (n = 208). Thirteen percent of such charges were for possession of less than one ounce of marijuana (n = 68) and 10 percent were for drinking in public (n = 54). Other less common charges included possession of drug paraphernalia or drugs, being a minor in possession of alcohol, being under the influence of drugs, and having an open alcohol container in public.

The fourth category of offenses involved violations of traditional criminal statutes, such as violent and property crimes and offenses against the public. This category included 379 offenses, of which one-third were for petty theft, usually shoplifting (n = 127). Twelve percent of such charges were for assault and battery (n = 46), 8 percent for providing false identification (n = 31), and 7 percent for trespassing (n = 27). Other less frequently occurring offenses included misdemeanor burglaries, prostitution, resisting arrest, excessive noise, vandalism, and possession of illegal weapons.

The remaining cases in our sample included offenses aimed at controlling the indigent (n = 52: loitering, illegal lodging for sleeping in parks, soliciting work without a permit, and urinating in public), business-related offenses (n = 14: maintaining a filthy restaurant, failure to have a fire extinguisher on premises, and maintaining a dangerous building), and those offenses that did not fit into the other five categories (n = 28: unlicensed or unleashed dogs, animals at the beach, skateboarding in prohibited areas, fishing without a license, and fueling a boat while docking).

RELIABILITY OF OUR SAMPLE AND GUILTY PLEAS

Our sample of offenders and their cases may not be representative of arraignment hearings in other courts in the same county or elsewhere in the country. The types of arrests the police make and cases that prosecutors choose to accept, for example, probably differ from one geographic area to another.

The sample on which this study is based may be idiosyncratic. One way to explore this possibility is to examine the types of offenders in our sample who pled guilty at their arraignments and compare them to the findings of earlier studies.

The vast majority (80–95%) of defendants at the misdemeanor court level enter pleas of guilty (Alfini, 1981; Brickey & Miller, 1975; Lindquist, 1988; McCall, 1978; Mileski, 1971; President's Commission Task Force Report on the Courts, 1967). Only 70 percent (n = 1,114) of defendants in our sample, however, entered pleas of guilty. One-fourth of the defendants (26%, n = 422) entered pleas of not guilty. The remaining cases were disposed of through continuances (3%, n = 44) and dropped charges (1%, n = 15).

The proportion of individuals in our sample who admitted guilt is a little low, given estimates by other researchers. There are, however, likely explanations for the disparity. Many of the defendants in our sample of arraignments may have entered "not guilty" pleas in order to bargain with prosecutors for lenient sentences in exchange for guilty pleas at later hearings, a frequent occurrence in criminal courts (Lindquist, 1988, p. 24). Our courtroom observers reported that some defendants were directed by the judges to enter pleas of not guilty because they would be, as one judge noted, "better off" seeing the district attorney before pleading guilty. We did not track those who pled not guilty, but it makes sense that a sizable portion later admitted guilt.

The low guilty plea rate among the individuals in our sample may be linked, in part, to the judges' desires to "do justice." Their orders to defendants to "negotiate" with the prosecutors falls within that framework. Further, some of the judges told defendants to plead not guilty and to obtain legal representation. One judge, for example, told a defendant to enter a not guilty plea and obtain counsel because he had a "good chance" of acquittal.

Our explanations for the low proportion of guilty pleas in our sample are plausible, but they raise a problem. The following analyses, which examine offender characteristics associated with pleading guilty, are limited in that we do not know which defendants might have later changed their pleas from "not guilty" to "guilty." The analyses represent, therefore, an investigation of people who plead guilty at arraignment and not necessarily a study of who pleads guilty.

Prior Record

Individuals who plead guilty may be more likely to be first-time offenders since defendants with prior criminal records may go to trial in order to avoid the expected harsher penalties imposed by judges on repeat offenders. As a result, our sample of judicial sentences may disproportionately exclude those assessed on repeat offenders.

Details on offenders' prior records were difficult for us to obtain because such information is often treated as confidential information by the courts. All of the judges in our sample made some attempt to provide us with this data, usually before imposing sentences, by announcing the number and type of priors defendants had. If offenders had no prior records, the judges did not make any statements or, in a few cases, indicated that the charges represented the offenders' first convictions.

Our method of collecting offenders' prior records was not without its drawbacks. When judges ordered penalties without indicating any previous criminal behavior, we could not always assume the offenders had no records because some judges simply forgot to indicate prior convictions. Sometimes, the judges apologized after a session for forgetting to mention defendants' criminal histories. In some instances, the judges may not have known the observers were present. One judge, for example, apologized after an observation session and told us that her bailiff had not notified her that our courtroom observers were collecting data. The observers, in such instances, did not always request defendants' prior records from court clerks or the judges due to the high number of cases heard in a session (routinely between 30 and 40). To ask members of the courtroom staff to spend more than a few minutes answering questions would have been awkward.

The very cooperative judges consistently provided us with information on prior records during the hearings. It was often the less cooperative judges who processed an entire session's cases without indicating that any of the defendants had previous convictions. We were able to ascertain whether some of these defendants had prior records based on the offenses for which they were arraigned (e.g., failure to pay a previously imposed fine means that the individual must have been convicted of some offense at an earlier date). But we were unable to determine whether other individuals arraigned during such sessions had been convicted of previous crimes.

We only included those cases where we could determine if defendants had prior convictions (n = 946) in our analyses of the effects of prior record on pleadings. About one-third (32%) of these defendants had no prior convictions (n = 306); the remaining 68% had been convicted of at least one earlier criminal offense (n = 640). The highest number of prior convictions for any one defendant was, to use the judge's words, "pages and pages."

For those defendants for whom we had information on prior record, there was no difference between recidivists and

first-time offenders in their likelihoods of pleading guilty—
28 percent of first-time offenders pled not guilty as opposed to
29 percent of those with prior records. Based upon these numbers, it seems unlikely that our sample of judicial sentences
disproportionately excluded those handed out to offenders
with criminal histories.[7]

Offense Severity

We expected that our sample disproportionately excluded
defendants who faced lengthy jail terms. We believed that
such individuals might plead not guilty in order to bargain
with prosecutors or opt for jury trials in hopes of avoiding
incarceration.

To examine whether our study systematically excluded
individuals accused of serious offenses, we recorded all the
charges against defendants announced by the judges. Possible
penalties were determined from state and municipal codes.
Almost all defendants, if convicted of the most serious offense
with which they were charged, could have been sentenced to
jail. The vast majority of cases (83%, n = 1,325) involved misdemeanors for which the maximum penalty was six months in
jail, a fine, or both. The most serious charge in 11 percent (n =
179) of the cases could have resulted in incarceration for one
year. The remaining cases involved offenses which could
result in ninety days in jail plus a fine (n = 31, 2%), or infractions for which the maximum penalty was a fine (n = 66, 4%).

We computed the "possible maximum sentence" for each
offender in our sample by summing the jail time each could
have received for each of the charges against them. For example, a defendant charged with driving on a suspended license
(maximum penalty of 6 months and a fine) and drunk in public (maximum 6 months and a fine) could receive a possible
maximum sentence of one year in jail plus a fine.

To examine whether offense seriousness affected guilty
pleas, we divided the defendants into two groups: those who
could receive one year or more in jail for having pled guilty to
the charges against them (n = 527), and those who faced less
severe sentences (n = 1,073).[8] This coding scheme closely par-

allels the division of criminal acts into felonies (punishable by incarceration for one year or more) and misdemeanors (punishable by less time, up to one year). Although all the offenses in our sample were misdemeanors, this approach allowed us to arrange the terms of incarceration into two logical groupings.

Those who faced serious charges were more likely to plead not guilty; 25 percent of those who faced less than one year in jail pled not guilty compared to 33 percent of those who confronted longer sentences (phi = .08, p < .001).[9] Clearly, defendants facing significant charges, because they were more likely to have pled not guilty at their arraignments, were disproportionately excluded from our sample of sentenced offenders.

Pretrial Detention

It may be that our sample does not accurately depict the world of individuals sentenced in municipal courts because it is not representative with respect to the proportion of defendants held in jail prior to their arraignments. Some researchers have argued that defendants held in custody are more likely to plead guilty, especially if, as a result, they expect to be released (e.g., Brickey & Miller, 1975). In such cases, pleading "not guilty" prolongs the time spent in jail awaiting trials.

We do not know the proportion of defendants in U.S. municipal courts who are held in jail prior to their arraignments.[10] But we can determine if in-custody defendants in our sample were more likely to plead guilty and therefore be overrepresented in the present study of judicial sentencing.

One-fifth of the defendants in our sample were detained prior to their arraignments (21%, n = 328); the remainder were at liberty (79%, n = 1267) or unable to be classified by our observers (n = 5). An equal proportion (about 75%) of in-custody and at liberty defendants pleaded guilty. But in-custody individuals who faced a year or more in jail were more likely to plead guilty than individuals who were at liberty and faced similar penalties (74% versus 62%; phi = .13, p < .01). Some at-liberty defendants may have pled not guilty in hopes of striking a better deal with prosecutors, while in-custody individuals in otherwise similar circumstances might have traded a plea of guilty for immediate freedom. Our finding adds to the evidence indicating that those in custody may plead guilty at higher rates than those who are at liberty. It also indicates that they are overrepresented in our study of judicial sentencing since our sample consists entirely of people who pleaded guilty at their arraignments.[11]

Number of Charges Defendants Faced

The number of charges defendants face may affect their probability of pleading guilty. Those facing many charges may be likely to plead "not guilty" in hopes that prosecutors may dismiss one or more charges in exchange for a guilty plea at a later date. If true, this could bias our sample of judicial decisions toward under inclusion of individuals who were charged with multiple crimes.

The majority of the defendants (61%, n = 981) in our sample were charged with one criminal violation. A quarter (n = 396) faced two charges and 14% (n = 221) had three or more charges. We could not determine the total number of charges against two defendants. The highest number of charges a single defendant faced was eleven. The number of crimes with which the individuals were charged did not appear to affect their likelihood of pleading guilty; roughly 70 percent of all groups admitted guilt.

Presence of Counsel

We expected that attorneys are generally retained by those facing more severe penalties because they may best benefit from assistance with their cases.[12] As anticipated, defendants who faced severe charges or who had past criminal convictions or both in combination were more likely to seek representation, probably because they might benefit most from it.[13]

Repeat offenders facing a year or more in jail were less likely to enter guilty pleas if they had attorneys; 55 percent of such offenders with attorneys pleaded guilty compared with 71 percent of their counterparts without defense counsel (phi =

.13, p = .05). Overall, those with attorneys were significantly less likely to enter guilty pleas; 73 percent of those without defense counsel pleaded guilty compared to only 64 percent of those with attorneys (phi = .06, p < .05). This fact further threatens the representativeness of our sample of judicial sentences since offenders with attorneys were systemically excluded.[14]

Defendant Ethnicity

Certain ethnic groups may be more likely to plead guilty. Maureen Mileski (1971), for example, found that blacks and "Spanish-Americans" were less likely than whites to admit guilt. If true, they may be underrepresented in our sample of judicially imposed penalties.

Defendant's ethnicity was noted by our courtroom observers during the arraignments. Since our observers did not have easy access to court records, they were forced to categorize defendants based on their names and appearances. In order to justify classification, the two observers had to agree regarding a defendant's ethnicity. This technique may be considered questionable due to the limits posed by observation. Direct scrutiny, however, has one strong advantage. If bias in sentencing exists, it may be based on how judges visually classify defendants rather than how they are identified on paper.

Nearly half (48%) of the defendants in our sample were determined by our observers to be white (n = 769); 40 percent were Hispanic (n = 655); 5 percent were black (n = 78); 4 percent were Asian (n = 70); and a combined 1 percent (n = 16) were Middle Eastern, Polynesian, or American Indian. Ethnicity was unavailable for twelve defendants because they sent attorneys to represent them at their arraignments.

Hispanics were more likely to admit culpability; 78 percent of them pleaded guilty compared to 69 percent of whites (phi = .10, p < .001). They admitted guilt more often even when we controlled for other matters, defendants' prior criminal records or the charges against them.[15] These matters meant that Hispanics are overrepresented in our study of judicial sentencing.

Fluency in English

The overrepresentation of Hispanics in our sample of sentenced offenders may be based on extralegal factors other than ethnicity. Some of these individuals were immigrants and were unable to communicate in English.[16] They came from countries where individuals are presumed guilty and must prove their innocence. They may have been confused by our court system and not understood that they might have bargained with prosecutors or had defense counsel provided for them. As a result, they may have been more likely to plead guilty at their arraignments—a matter we attempted to determine.

Our observers classified defendants as non-English-speaking if they required a translator or if they appeared to be unable to communicate in English. Three-quarters (n = 1,174) of the defendants in our sample appeared to be proficient in English. Most individuals who did not speak English spoke only Spanish (89%, n = 369), 8 percent (n = 32) spoke Asian languages (e.g., Vietnamese and Cantonese), and 3 percent (n = 7) spoke other languages (e.g., French). We were unable to determine the English proficiency for eighteen defendants, some of whom were absent from their arraignments.

English speakers were less likely to plead guilty than those who could not speak the language; 71 percent of the English speakers pleaded guilty compared to 78 percent of those who were not English proficient (phi = .07, p < .01).[17] The consequence for our study was that non-English speakers were overrepresented in our sample of judicial decisions. Due to Southern California's melting-pot nature, any study of the municipal courts conducted there will encounter a high proportion of non-English-speakers, which may threaten the generalizability of the study to other parts of the United States.

Defendant Gender

Males are generally overrepresented in crime statistics and that was the case for our original sample of sixteen hundred: 84 percent (n = 1,336) were male, 16 percent (n = 262) were female. We were unable to determine the gender of two defendants who sent attorneys to represent them in absentia.[18] Men and women were equally likely to plead guilty and be included in our analyses of judicial decisions.[19]

Court-Related Charges

Facing court-related charges (e.g., failure to appear in court or pay an ordered fine) may increase defendants' fatalistic views of their courtroom outcomes since they cannot effectively deny the offenses with which they have been charged. Due to this sense of predetermined destiny they may be hesitant to plead not guilty. We found that this may be true; 80 percent of those charged with court related offenses pled guilty compared to only 69 percent of those facing other charges (phi = .12, p < .0001). When we controlled for offense severity and prior record, the relationship held; those charged with court related offenses remained more likely to plead guilty.[20] This indicates that our sample of judicial sentences disproportionately includes those imposed on defendants facing court related charges.

MULTIVARIATE ANALYSIS OF GUILTY PLEAS

To determine which factors were most associated with the entering of guilty pleas, and thus gain a more complete picture of how these factors affected our sample of judicial sentences, we conducted a logistic regression analysis.[21]

Logistic regression determines the association between a dependent variable and each of the independent variables while "controlling" for the effects of the other independent variables. Logistic regression is an advanced statistical technique, but has limitations. Of most consideration here is its requirement that only cases with complete information be included in the analyses. Defendants for whom we were unable to determine prior records, for example, were excluded from this examination. Their exclusion drastically reduced the sample size from 1,600 to 943 and may have resulted in some findings that differ from those we have already reported in the previous pages (which we will discuss).

The legal variables we incorporated into our equations included: seriousness of offense (one year or more in jail = 1, less than a year = 0), prior record (prior convictions = 1, no prior convictions = 0), number of charges (the actual number of charges), and whether the offender was in custody at arraignment (in custody = 1, at liberty = 0). Extralegal characteristics of the defendants included: ethnicity[22] (white = 1, nonwhite = 0), fluency in English (fluent in English = 1, not fluent = 0), and gender (male = 1, female = 0). We also included the presence of counsel (attorney present = 1, no counsel present = 0). Results are shown in Table 4.1.

As expected, the severity of the defendants' crimes and their prior records affected whether they admitted guilt. Defendants who faced one year or more in jail were one-third as likely to plead guilty as those who faced less time (OR = .36, p < .0001). Repeat offenders were two-thirds as likely as first-

TABLE 4.1
Logistic Regression Analysis Predicting Guilty Pleas

Variable	β	SE	df	Prob.	Odds ratio
facing year or more	−1.013	.226	1	.000	.363
prior record	−.431	.191	1	.024	.650
number of charges	.015	.099	1	.878	1.015
white offender	−.226	.190	1	.233	.798
fluent in English	−.414	.229	1	.071	.661
male offender	.271	.218	1	.214	1.312
attorney present	−.040	.338	1	.906	.961
appeared in custody	−.247	.253	1	.329	.781
court related charges	1.373	.217	1	.000	3.947
constant	1.986	.531	1	.000	

Summary statistics	χ^2	df	Prob.
−2 log likelihood	980.175	891	.020
Model χ^2	66.313	9	.000
Improvement	66.313	9	.000
Goodness of fit	886.845	891	.533

Note: Percentage of correct dependent variable classification by model is 72.70 percent.

time offenders to enter guilty pleas (OR = .65, p < .05). It appears that those who have the most to lose are more likely to hold out for a plea bargain or take their chances at trial.

Our other legal variables, number of charges and appearance in custody, were not related to defendants' likelihoods of pleading guilty in this analysis. Those who appeared in custody were equally as likely as their free counterparts to plead guilty (OR = .78, n.s.), possibly indicating that those in custody do not plead guilty to get out of jail more rapidly once other variables have been controlled. Our earlier finding that in-custody individuals who faced a year or more in jail were more likely to plead guilty than individuals who were at liberty and faced similar sentences may have disappeared in the multivariate model because such individuals were only a small part of the overall sample (n = 226).

Those charged with court-related offenses were nearly four times as likely as defendants charged with other types of offenses to plead guilty (OR = 3.95, p < .0001). This finding is most likely based on the difficulties of pleading not guilty to indisputable charges such as failure to appear and failure to comply with previously imposed sanctions, such as community service orders or fines. Defendants may simply accept their fates and plead guilty.

None of our extralegal defendant characteristics were significantly associated with pleading guilty once other factors had been controlled. These findings indicate that in our sample defendant characteristics played a minimal role in most defendants' decisions to plead guilty.

Based on the above analyses, determinations to enter guilty pleas were grounded on legal factors. In this regard, it seems unlikely that our sample's decision-making differs from what takes place in other U.S. municipal courts. In the next chapter, we examine the association between legal, extralegal, and organizational factors and the sentences imposed by judges on those who pled guilty.

CHAPTER 5

THE PROCESS OF DOING JUSTICE: WHAT THE JUDGES DID

In this chapter we explore the multitude of factors that may influence judicial sentencing. We begin with the assumption that judges, as all humans, possess attitudes that favor some people over others and that occasionally such opinions affect their behavior. We are interested in learning defendant characteristics and courtroom circumstances that may give rise to such bias. Such items include legal, extralegal, and organizational variables.

The punishments the judges gave to those defendants who pleaded guilty varied greatly, but for the most part, appeared related to their illegal activities and prior criminal records. Fines were the most common sanction. Nearly one-half of the 1,120 sentenced offenders left their arraignments less some cash.[1] The figure would have been higher, but some judges granted defendants requests to substitute community service for financial penalties they could not afford.[2]

As a group, the judges were more likely than justices noted elsewhere to send people to jail (Feeley, 1979, p. 137; Mileski, 1971; Ryan, 1980–81). Nearly a third of the offenders in our sample received a jail sentence (31%, n = 345). Half of the sentences were for ten days or less; only 20 percent of the jail terms exceeded thirty days in length, only 5 percent surpassed ninety days. Still, these numbers are near the highest reported rate for a study of misdemeanor courts (35% in Ryan's 1980–81 inquiry).

The high degree of incarceration is particularly notable since defendants in our original sample of sixteen hundred who faced long jail terms had disproportionately pleaded not guilty at their arraignments and so were not included in the judicial sentences we report here. It is reasonable to assume that their eventual punishments would have raised the frequency of incarceration. The more extensive use of jail by the judges in the present study may be the result of mandatory jail sentences that did not exist at the time of earlier studies or the conservative political nature of the county under study.

In all, 16 percent of the offenders in our sample were sentenced to perform community service (n = 174). A small percentage (n = 35, 3%) were given the opportunity to participate in diversion programs.[3] The remainder of the sample received lesser penalties, usually probation.[4]

THE EFFECT OF LEGAL VARIABLES ON JUDGES' SENTENCING

Legal variables, such as prior record and the seriousness and number of charges against defendants, are "those which the system may legitimately use to fix sentences" (Lizotte, 1978, p. 567). Such characteristics have been shown to be associated with punishment severity. Harsher sentences, for example, are consistently given to those convicted of more severe offenses (Green, 1964; Lizotte, 1978; Myers, 1987; Myers & Talarico, 1988; Petersilia & Turner, 1985; Uhlman, 1977; 1979). The judges we interviewed also told us that these legal factors were important in their sentencing and we expected to see this reflected in our analyses of their decisions.

Seriousness of Offense

We used the longest terms to which defendants might be sentenced as a measure of the seriousness of their crimes.[5] Based on this, the severity of their offenses did affect defendants' punishments. Those who faced at least one year in custody were significantly more likely to be sent to jail than transgressors who confronted less time.[6] Over half (58%) of those looking at a year or more in lock-up were actually sentenced to jail compared to 19 percent of those whose possible maximum sentences involved less than twelve months (phi = .38, p < .0001).

Another measure of offense seriousness is the number of charges against defendants. Lawbreakers charged with multiple offenses may be punished more harshly than their counterparts who are charged with fewer crimes (Klein, Ebener, Abrahamse, & Fitzgerald, 1991; Green, 1961). Indeed, the judges told us that they consider those who are guilty of many offenses to be more culpable, a point supported by our results. The judges' sentencing decisions were affected by total number of charges, but only if the possible maximum sentence was a year or more; such defendants were significantly more likely to be sent to jail if they faced multiple charges (phi = .28, p < .0001).[7]

Prior Record

Research has shown that recidivists are sanctioned more severely than first-time offenders (e.g., Berger, 1976; Lindquist, 1988, p. 171; Mileski, 1971; Spohn, 1990; Uhlman, 1979), and the judges we interviewed told us that they were more likely to jail offenders who had histories of criminal activities. They were true to their word. Repeat offenders were more likely to be sentenced to confinement; nearly half (47%) went to jail compared to only 5 percent of those without previous convictions (phi = .42, p < .0001).[8] Individuals with prior records who faced possible maximum sentences of a year or more were almost five times as likely to be incarcerated compared to individuals in similar circumstances who had no prior records (66% versus 14%). The disparity was even greater for defendants who confronted terms of less than a year.[9]

Our finding that prior record affects sentence severity supports the judges' statements that they consider those with prior records to be unlikely candidates for rehabilitation. The judges, as evidenced by their increased reliance on jail sentences, were more likely to feel that incapacitation, retribution, or deterrence were the more appropriate punishment responses for these individuals.

Pretrial Detention

Pretrial detention has been associated with higher chances of conviction and more serious penalties (Knowles & Prewitt, 1969). For our sample, the seriousness of the charges they faced and their prior records determined the likelihood of defendants appearing in custody at their arraignments.[10] Not surprisingly, because these legal variables also influence sentence severity, appearance in custody was related to the severity of sentences imposed on the offenders in our sample. Offenders who were in custody at the time of their sentencing (n = 232) were likely to remain in jail; 86 percent were detained while only 16 percent of those who did not appear in custody were jailed (phi = .61, p < .0001).[11]

EFFECTS OF EXTRALEGAL CHARACTERISTICS ON SENTENCING

Extralegal attributes of offenders are not necessarily associated with offenses, but are rather demographic information about offenders. For our analyses, we collected information on defendants' ethnicity, gender, and English proficiency. Judicial sentencing may be considered biased if it is affected by such defendant characteristics. Research on these matters is inconclusive. Some studies find no evidence of bias while others indicate that it exists (see Chapter 2 for a review of this literature).

Offender Race

The influence of defendant's race/ethnicity on judicial sentencing is the most often researched extralegal defendant characteristic. The literature may be divided into two camps, although the two camps' findings often overlap. One set of researchers claims that race/ethnicity is, under certain conditions, a contributing factor in the sentencing behavior of judges (e.g., Lizotte, 1978; Meeker et al., 1992; Myers, 1987; Smith, 1987), while other investigators maintain that legal variables, not race nor ethnicity, account for observed punishment disparities (e.g., Green, 1964; Kleck, 1981; 1985).

Researchers studying the effects of racial bias on judicial sentencing have often combined all minority groups into one category, "nonwhites." We did likewise and found that they were more likely than whites to be sent to jail regardless of the severity of their crimes.[12] But when we also considered previous criminal convictions, the disparity in sentences between the two groups disappeared. This finding supports the results of those who posit that judicially imposed penalties are not based on one's ethnicity.

We considered the possibility that the category "nonwhite" does not disentangle biases that are presumed to exist in society. It has been noted, for example, that Asians, who were included in our "nonwhite" category, are viewed more favorably by the majority population than are other minorities (Jesilow, Geis, Song, & Pontell, 1992) and may be treated differently. Indeed, Asians in our sample were punished with jail less often than were whites (20% compared to 25%). We decided to exclude them as well as Middle Easterners, Polynesians, and Native Americans from our reanalysis (because of their small numbers).

Blacks and Hispanics, whether considered separately or grouped together were more often sentenced to jail, but the results were not statistically significant; one quarter of white offenders were sent to jail, while 36 percent of Hispanics and 36 percent of blacks received incarceration (phi = .001, n.s). But when the possible maximum sentence was a year or more, half of the white offenders were incarcerated; blacks went to jail 57 percent of the time; and 66 percent of Hispanics were sentenced to jail (phi = .19, p < .05).[13] The addition of prior record to the analyses did not change the direction of the results; we found that whites were still less likely to be incarcerated than blacks and Hispanics (although the few number of cases we had may have precluded statistically significant results).[14] These results support the argument that ethnicity may have some effect on sentencing, and that research on judicial bias that lumps all minorities into one category may mask inequities.

Offender's Fluency in English

Despite our results, we were not convinced that ethnicity was the primary cause of the disparity between the sentencing of whites and some minorities, predominately Hispanics. During our interviews, the judges told us that non-English-speaking defendants take extra court time and pose additional problems for the courts because they require translators.[15] Our observers also noted that non-English speakers required additional efforts, which sometimes frustrated the judges. For example, one translator could not be found, causing the judge to yell for someone to find him so the defendant's hearing could begin. Another judge began questioning a defendant who appeared without representation before his interpreter could be located; when the interpreter arrived, she was noticeably upset that the judge had questioned a defendant who was known to need an interpreter. We wanted to determine if this extra burden may have biased judges' sentencing decisions against these offenders.

Fluency in English appeared to affect punishments for the offenders in our sample. English speakers were significantly less likely to be sent to jail than those who spoke only foreign languages (phi = .10, p < .001). Moreover, we found that non-English speakers, whether or not they had prior records or faced long terms of incarceration, were significantly more likely to be sentenced to jail than their English speaking counterparts.[16] The effect of language on judicial sentencing was most pronounced for Hispanic offenders. Illustrative is the fate of those with prior records who faced one year or more in jail. Hispanics who spoke English (n = 30) had about an equal chance of drawing a jail term or being released. Non-English-speaking Hispanics (n = 41), on the other hand, were incarcerated 85 percent of the time (phi = .35, p < .01).

These results suggest that language, rather than ethnicity, is the factor associated with judicial penalties. Language, however, is probably just an indicator of cultural differences. That is, defendants whose language, dress, attitudes, or mannerisms substantially differ from the majority population's may be treated differentially. Not being able to speak English is probably found in common with other culturally determined characteristics.

In addition, other problems may exist for defendants who do not speak English. As one judge told us:

A judge who does not speak the language has to rely on the interpreter, and that interpreter may be a very good interpreter, but it does not allow for assessment of credibility, it does not allow for assessment of demeanor, for assessment of things that are intangible.

Offender Gender

Most research on the effects of defendant gender on sentence severity has found that female offenders are treated less harshly than their male counterparts (Daly, 1994; Meeker et al., 1992, although Martha Myers [1987] found that females received longer sentences than males in the state of Georgia). We add to this evidence.

Males, in almost all instances, were significantly more likely than females to receive jail sentences (phi = .12, p < .0001). The one exception was with respect to repeat offenders facing incarceration of a year or more. Here, females were equally as likely as males to go to jail (66% of males and 61% of females in this category were incarcerated). It may well be that the justices, based on what they told us during the interviews, perceived these women as unlikely to benefit from leniency. The severity of their crimes and prior records lead the judges to classify these female offenders in the same manner as they did their male counterparts.

Variables Relating to Judicial Characteristics

Many studies have examined the relationships between offender characteristics and sentencing, but ignored the characteristics of the judges who assigned penalties. They treat judges as if they "are interchangeable" (McCall, 1978, p. 120) and assume that judges sentence in a similar fashion due to base similarities they all share. Research, however, offers little support for the contention that judges do not vary much from each other; studies indicate that judges are, in fact, "complex" individuals (Wice, 1985, p. 99). Indeed, our interviews with the magistrates demonstrated their disparate views. Judicial diversity may explain some of the differences in their sentencing behaviors. To examine the relationships between characteristics of the judges and the punishments they handed out, we collected information on their ethnicities, genders, primary sentencing philosophies, and prejudicial careers.[17]

Judges' Ethnicities

The race of judges may be associated with sentencing decisions. Malcolm Holmes and colleagues (Holmes, Hosch, Daudistel, Perez, & Graves, 1993), for example, found that while white and Hispanic judges did not differ in their treatment of Hispanic defendants, white judges sentenced white defendants more leniently. Cassia Spohn (1990) also found that judicial race affected sentence severity; black judges in her sample were less likely than white judges to incarcerate offenders.

We collected data in the courtrooms of ten white judges and two nonwhite judges. The white judges were significantly more likely to sentence offenders to jail than their nonwhite counterparts. The white judges incarcerated 32 percent of the offenders before them, while the nonwhite judges jailed only 20 percent (phi = .10, p < .01). Neither offense severity nor prior records changed the relationship between judicial race and sentence severity. White judges used jail more often than did nonwhites in all circumstances.[18]

The fact that white judges sentenced offenders differently than did the nonwhite justices supports the belief that judges' individual characteristics affect their sentencing decisions. This analysis, however, does not disaggregate the effects of the judges' characteristics. Rather, it lumps all white judges and all nonwhite judges into two categories. The effect of even one or two "hanging" judges could easily bias our findings.

To explore the possibility that justices who have deviant punishment policies might have biased our results, we excluded from our analyses the two judges with the highest rates of incarceration (one was male and one was female; both were white). One judge sentenced everyone (n = 15) to jail and the other incarcerated 93 percent of those who pled guilty (n = 133). The next highest incarceration rate was 66 percent and the average for the entire judge sample was 31 percent.[19] One of the excluded judges told us she sentenced so many people to jail because she opposed the use of community service and felt the purpose of sentencing was to punish offenders, while the other excluded judge told us his primary role in the criminal justice system was the protection of society (which could be satisfied by jailing criminals).

When the two outlier judges were excluded from the analysis of the affects of judicial ethnicity on sentence severity, all differences between the groups disappeared. White and nonwhite judges sentenced about 20 percent of offenders to jail. Half of offenders with prior records who faced possible maximum sentences of a year or more were sent to jail by both groups. It appears that bias may lie with individual justices whose sentencing practices are far from the norm.

Ethnic Concordance

By default, early studies of racial bias in judicial sentencing focused on the sanctioning of minorities by white judges since they were conducted prior to the entrance of appreciable numbers of minorities into the judiciary. By ignoring the ethnicity of the judge and offender, it is conceivable that studies of more recent samples of justices might conclude that there are no racial effects on sentencing when, in fact, they exist. This would occur if judges were lenient with those whose ethnicity was the same as theirs. For example, the sentencing patterns of black judges who severely sentence whites might be erased in aggregate statistics by white judges who severely sentence blacks.

To determine if there was an ethnic bias in favor of those like oneself, we compared the judges' sentencing decisions with whether or not the judge and offender were the same ethnicity (ethnic concordance). In general, the judges did show some favoritism (phi = .07, p < .05). The disparity, however, hardly seems meaningful since only two of the judges were minority members and together they sentenced only nine same-ethnic offenders.

We decided to examine how white judges treated white (n = 458) versus nonwhite offenders (n = 489). Such an analysis is not new. Most recently, Holmes and colleagues (1993) found that white judges treated white offenders more leniently than they treated nonwhites. Our sample acted similarly; 27 percent of white offenders were jailed by white judges compared to 38 percent of nonwhite offenders (phi = .12, p < .001). This finding did not change with the consideration of the severity of the offenders' crimes or their prior records. White judges were still less likely to jail white offenders.[20]

There is one caveat to the finding that our white judges favored white defendants. After we factored in prior record, white defendants remained less likely than nonwhites to be incarcerated by white judges. The results, however, were statistically significant for only those repeat offenders who faced less than one year in jail; 31 percent of such offenders who were white were jailed by white judges compared to 45 percent of their nonwhite counterparts (phi = .15, p < .05). This, on the one hand, may indicate that the effect of ethnic concordance on the sentencing decisions of white judges diminishes when offenders' criminality is clear, since defendants with prior records who faced long terms were treated similarly. On the other hand, repeat offenders charged with less serious offenses could be considered less culpable than some other offenders and therefore, jail is not inevitable for them. Lemert and Rosberg (1948), for example, found that judges "downgraded" the criminality of white offenders. It may be that downgrading occurs where judges are less certain of the appropriate sentence, thus allowing other factors (e.g., sympathy for those who are like oneself) to enter into sentencing decisions.

Judicial Gender

Judges' gender may play a much bigger role than ethnicity in the formation of sentencing decisions. Men and women, at least according to prevailing wisdom, do have different ways of looking at the world. But a belief that women are the gentler of the sexes is not supported by our initial analysis; female judges were significantly more likely than their male counterparts to send people to jail. Female judges incarcerated 37 percent of their offenders compared with only 24 percent for male judges (phi = .14, p < .0001).

The sentencing disparity between male and female judges occurred with offenders who were the "most" criminal. First-time offenders, on the one hand, were very unlikely to be jailed by either male or female judges. On the other hand, repeat offenders facing serious charges fared better when sentenced by male judges; one-half of such offenders were incarcerated if they faced a male judge, but female justices sent three-quarters of those they saw to jail (phi = .25, p < .01).[21]

We hypothesized that the effect of judicial gender might disappear once we excluded our two "hanging judges" from the analyses. This had been the case when we left them out of the analyses on judicial race. Indeed, when we excluded our two outliers, the affect of judicial gender on sentencing disappeared; male and female judges sentenced 21 percent of the offenders before them to jail. It appears that the findings regarding judicial gender and incarceration rates were driven, at least in part, by judges whose sentencing decisions lie outside the norm established by their brethren. There is also the distinct possibility that the apparent harshness of the female judges was due to our inability to control for all conditions.

Gender Concordance

Interest in how offenders' gender affects their punishments is not new. Two experts (Myers & Talarico, 1988), for example, reported that female felons were sentenced more leniently by male judges than female judges. This was not the case in our study. Male judges were more merciful with male offenders, and female justices were more favorable to female defendants (phi = .21, p < .0001). Once again, the distinctions were noticeable with offenders who appeared "criminal." Male and female judges were unlikely to incarcerate people whose possible maximum sentence was less than one year, but when offenders confronted a year or more in jail, male judges incarcerated 35 percent of the men and 67 percent of the women, while female judges jailed 53 percent of male offenders and 46 percent of females. This situation did not change when we considered the prior records of offenders facing long terms; male judges still sentenced males more leniently than female offenders and female judges still treated females better than male offenders (phi = .35 p < .0001).

We thought that our measurement of a same-gender bias might be due to our outliers (those two judges who incarcerated very high proportions of offenders). The relationship, however, was still present and significant after we excluded the outliers from our analysis. Our finding that judge-offender gender dyads are associated with sentencing patterns suggests a gender bias not normally studied—judicial chauvinism by both sexes.

Prejudicial Careers

Another characteristic of judges that might affect their sentencing decisions is their prejudicial careers. Levin (1977, p. 91), for example, argued that their prejudicial careers explained why judges were more lenient in Pittsburgh than in Minneapolis. The Minneapolis judges, who came from private legal practice and had done little public service, were more likely to be society oriented and give more severe sentences than the Pittsburgh judges, who came from positions in political parties and government. Judges' social backgrounds, then, affected their sentencing decisions. In particular, magistrates' prior experiences as prosecutors may result in more severe sentences for offenders (Myers & Talarico, 1988, p. 112; Wice, 1985, p. 102).

Prior courtroom roles held by each judge in our study were noted during interviews with the justices or learned from their executive secretaries. Eight of the twelve judges had prejudicial careers as prosecutors; four held other positions.[22]

Judges who had prior roles as prosecutors were significantly more likely to send offenders to jail; they incarcerated 34 percent of offenders compared with only 21 percent jailed by other judges (phi = .13, p < .0001). The severity of the defendants' crimes did not affect the sentencing pattern, but the addition of prior records to our analysis eliminated the differences between the two groups; former prosecutors were not significantly more likely to impose jail. Moreover, when we excluded the outliers (both were former prosecutors) from all the analyses, all statistical differences between sentences imposed by judges who were prosecutors or those who held other prejudicial careers disappeared. This suggests that sentencing bias by former prosecutors may be limited to a few judges who often utilize jail.

Punishment Philosophy

In a system that allocates the "bulk of sentencing discretion" to judges (Berger, 1976, p. 52), individual differences in philosophies may play an important role in sentencing outcomes. Every judge brings to each case attitudes regarding offense severity, sentencing options, and punishment (Hood & Sparks, 1970, p. 152). Sentencing or punishment philosophies, then, may be an important consideration in determining judicial sentencing.

The judges' sentencing philosophies were learned during our interviews with them. Many of the judges (9 of the 12) told us they used more than one philosophy. We coded the first one they told us as their primary sentencing ideology. We assumed that the first philosophy they mentioned was paramount in their minds and the one that most often influenced their sentencing.

Forty percent of the offenders were sentenced by judges who told us their primary sentencing philosophy was incapacitation; 23 percent were sentenced by rehabilitation-oriented justices; 20 percent were sentenced by retribution-oriented judges; and 17 percent were sentenced by justices who told us their primary sentencing philosophy was deterrence.

Offenders who were sentenced by judges who told us retribution was their primary sentencing philosophy were significantly more likely to be incarcerated than offenders sentenced by judges who said they employed other philosophies; retribution-oriented judges had an incarceration rate of 62 percent compared to 20 percent for deterrence-oriented judges; 21 percent for incapacitation-oriented justices; and, 27 percent for rehabilitation-oriented magistrates (Cramer's V = .35, p < .0001). Offenders, whose possible maximum sentences were less than one year in jail, were unlikely to be sent to jail.[23] But the retribution-oriented judges sent to jail 39 percent of such offenders (Cramer's V = .21, p < .0001). Defendants facing more than one year in jail fared much worse. Judges with retribution on their minds jailed 87 percent of these offenders whom they sentenced. By contrast, rehabilitation-oriented justices incarcerated 51 percent of this group, while deterrence and incapacitation-oriented judges jailed about 40 percent (Cramer's V = .42, p < .0001).

The addition of prior records to our analyses did not change the results. Retribution-oriented judges, for example, incarcerated 92 percent of repeat offenders facing one year or more in jail compared to an incarceration rate of about one-half for the other judges (Cramer's V = .43, p < .0001).[24]

Obviously, the magistrates, who told us that their primary punishment philosophy was retribution sentenced offenders to jail much more often than did the other judges.[25] They disdained the use of community-based punishments (probation and community service), seemingly because they believed that jail time was necessary to satisfy retribution.

We wanted to determine if the retribution-oriented judges sentenced evenly all ethnicities that came before them. Cesare Beccaria (1775/1983) expressed the belief that when sentences are severe they are more likely to be used against weaker individuals, and that leniency will be granted to those of more normal means. To test this assumption, we compared the treatment of white and Hispanic offenders and found that Hispanic repeat offenders were treated more harshly than their white counterparts by retribution-oriented judges.[26] All Hispanic offenders facing one year or more in jail (n = 35) who were sentenced by retribution-oriented judges were incarcerated. The same justices sent to jail 79 percent of such white offenders (n = 19, phi = .38, p < .0001). Hispanic repeat offenders facing less serious charges were also more likely to be sentenced to incarceration by retribution-oriented judges (61% of Hispanics versus 32% of whites, phi = .29, p < .05). Such significant differences in ethnic sentencing were not found for judges who employed other primary sentencing philosophies. As Beccaria suggested, heavy-handed justice may lead to unequal treatment.

The Effects of Organizational Factors
on Judicial Sentencing

Sentencing by judges may be affected by a third class of factors that are associated with the operation of the courtroom (see Chapter 2). We are only able to comment on two of these organizational characteristics: the length of defendants' hearings and whether they were represented by counsel.

Length of Hearing

Organizational theorists argue that defendants who usurp the court's time are penalized as judges retaliate with harsher sentences (Blumberg, 1967; Eisenstein & Jacob, 1977; Mileski, 1971; Nardulli, 1978). To ascertain whether the duration of hearings was associated with sentencing, our observers timed the arraignments.[27] All the arraignments were relatively short (from a few seconds to fifteen minutes), but in these fast-paced courtrooms even a few minutes seemed slow as justices rushed to complete their work loads.

Offenders with lengthy hearings (4 or more minutes) were more likely to be sent to jail than defendants who spent less time before the bar (Cramer's V = .12, p < .001).[28] This finding held when offense seriousness was considered; those with long hearings were still more likely to be incarcerated than those with shorter arraignments. The addition to the analyses of the defendants' past criminal records did not alter matters substantially. Repeat offenders facing less than a year in jail were more likely to be incarcerated if their arraignments were elongated; 33 percent of such offenders with short hearings were sent to jail compared to 42 percent of their counterparts with intermediate hearings and 67 percent of similar offenders with lengthy hearings (Cramer's V = .17, p < .05).[29] For repeat offenders facing less than a year in jail, incarceration may be associated with taking the court's time. The more time cases take, the higher the chances of jail.

The one exception to the association between the length of arraignments and jail sentences occurred with repeat offenders facing one year or more in custody. Offenders with intermediate hearings were least likely to be incarcerated; 54 percent of such defendants with intermediate hearings ended up in jail, while 71 percent of such offenders with short hearings and 78 percent of their counterparts with protracted hearings were incarcerated. This nonlinear association indicates that the likelihood of jail may be based on factors other than hearing length. It is possible that incarceration resulted from serious allegations of two types: those whose guilt was clearly established early in the hearing, and those whose level of culpability required some questioning and presentation of evidence. Indeed, a few of our observers noted that lengthy hearings were the results of judges questioning defendants about their actions and attorneys reading key parts of the files to the judges.

Presence of Legal Counsel

It is standard wisdom that defendants do better in court if they have legal representation, and the presence of counsel has been a point of interest to researchers studying sentencing (Blumberg, 1967; Knowles & Prewitt, 1969; Mileski, 1971; Uhlman, 1979, Wice, 1985). It was, therefore, surprising to us that offenders in our sample who were represented by attorneys (either private or public) were sent to jail more often than those who did not appear with counsel.[30]

Our analysis of the relationship between having an attorney and one's punishment was based on the belief that counsel affected punishments. We decided to turn the matter on its head; the potential for severe punishments caused defendants to obtain lawyers. For example, individuals who faced lesser charges or a low probability of incarceration were probably less likely to believe they needed an attorney. Indeed, no first-time offenders and only fifteen recidivists who faced less than one year in jail had defense counsel.

We decided to examine whether having an attorney was an outcome of the seriousness of offenders' crimes and prior records, our legal measures. As expected, defendants who faced severe charges or who had past criminal convictions or both in combination were more likely to seek representation, probably because they might benefit most from it.[31]

Representation by counsel does not appear to be a haphazard decision. Rather, it appears that those who have the most to lose are most likely to obtain an attorney to assist them in their dealings with the criminal courts. Our analysis, however, tells us nothing about the effect of legal representation on sentencing.

There is one noteworthy exception to our finding that obtaining counsel is associated with defendants' realizations that they may go to jail. Defendants who were not fluent in English were significantly less likely to be represented by any form of counsel.[32] They may have been unaware of their rights to defense counsel. It is also possible, although unlikely, that some of the non-English-speaking defendants mistook their translators for attorneys.[33]

MULTIVARIATE ANALYSIS OF JUDICIAL USE OF INCARCERATION

In order to determine which factors were "most" associated with judges' use of incarceration, we employed logistic regression, an analysis which examines each factor while controlling for each of the other variables. Because this type of analysis excludes any case for which one does not have complete information, only 667 cases (rather than 1,114) were included for study. Every statistical technique has its limitations and logistic regression is no exception. Because of this qualification, results obtained from the logistic regression analysis may differ from those obtained in our previous analyses.

To determine whether the sample used in the logistic regression differed in composition from the sample used in the analyses reported above, we compared the composition of the crosstabulation samples to the reduced sample used in the logistic regression. The samples were not significantly different with respect to the variables of interest,[34] with one exception. Offenders sentenced by male judges were overrepresented in the sample used for the logistic regression (42% of the cross tabulation sample were sentenced by male judges versus 47% of the sample used for the logistic regression; phi = .05, p < .01).

We entered into the logistic regression equation the legal and extralegal variables and organizational factors that we found to be associated with judicial use of incarceration during our earlier analyses. The legal variables we incorporated into our equations included: seriousness of offense, prior record, number of charges, and whether the offender was in custody at arraignment. Extralegal characteristics of the defendant included: ethnicity (white versus nonwhite),[35] fluency in English, and gender. Extralegal characteristics of the judge included: judge's ethnicity (white versus nonwhite), gender, and primary sentencing philosophy (retribution versus others). (Due to concerns about multicollinearity, prejudicial career, gender concordance, and ethnic concordance were excluded from the multivariate analysis.[35]) Organizational variables included: length of hearing (short versus intermediate versus lengthy), and presence of counsel. Results are shown in Table 5.2.

As predicted, there was a significant independent effect for prior record; those with prior records were twenty-two times more likely to be incarcerated than first-time offenders (OR = 22.5, p < .0001). There was also a significant effect for appearance in custody; offenders who were in custody were nearly fifty-four times more likely to be sent to jail than those who were not detained before trial (OR = 53.9, p < .0001). The number of charges also significantly affected the likelihood of jail; for each additional charge offenders faced, their odds of incarceration increased by a factor of 1.6 (OR = 1.6, p < .05). Taken together, it is clear that these three legal variables were important factors in judges' decisions to impose jail terms.

Our fourth legal variable, offense severity, was not associated with likelihood of incarceration in this model (OR = .84, n.s.). The effects for this variable disappeared when our other variables were included in the model. It is most likely that our other variables were more important in predicting whether a given offender would be sent to jail. This finding, however, may also be due to the fact that the logistic regression analysis only included those cases for which we had information on all the variables included in the equation, which

TABLE 5.2
Logistic Regression Analysis Predicting Incarceration

Variable	β	SE	df	Prob.	Odds ratio
facing year or more	−.1773	.363	1	.625	.838
prior record	3.1145	.431	1	.000	22.522
white offender	.1193	.288	1	.678	1.127
fluent in English	−1.1784	.323	1	.000	.308
male offender	−.0731	.376	1	.846	.930
white judge	−.7235	.705	1	.305	.485
male judge	1.2503	.627	1	.046	3.492
retribution-oriented	.9516	.638	1	.136	2.590
hearing length	.6362	.188	1	.001	1.889
attorney present	−1.1989	.695	1	.085	.302
appeared in custody	3.9874	.566	1	.000	53.915
number of charges	.4896	.196	1	.012	1.632
constant	−7.1341	.999	1	.000	

Summary statistics	χ^2	df	Prob.
−2 log likelihood	473.418	615	1.000
Model χ^2	321.343	12	.000
Improvement	321.343	12	.000
Goodness of fit	556.189	615	.957

Note: Percentage of correct dependent variable classification by model is 81.85 percent.

reduced the sample size and the likelihood of statistical significance.

Offenders who were not fluent in English were three times as likely as English speakers to be jailed (OR = .31, p < .0001). It appears that non-English speakers were penalized for the extra burdens they put on the court system. It must be noted that the logistic regression analysis statistically controlled the possible associations between fluency in English and other variables (e.g., prior record or offense severity). Therefore, language proficiency was associated with the judges' decisions to incarcerate separately from any of the legal variables we measured.

Our other extralegal offender characteristics did not significantly affect the judges' decisions to incarcerate. Offenders' ethnicity and gender did not consistently affect the likelihoods of jail; nonwhites were equally as likely as whites (OR = 1.1, n.s.) to be incarcerated as were males and females (OR = .93, n.s.). The presumed effects for these two characteristics (ethnicity and gender) virtually disappeared when other factors were considered in this analysis, indicating that extralegal offender attributes, for the most part, may have had little affect on judges' decisions to use jail.

One judicial characteristic significantly affected the likelihood of jail. Offenders sentenced by male judges were three and a half times as likely to be incarcerated than those sentenced by female judges when our other factors were controlled (OR = 3.5, p < .05). A number of explanations are possible. As we noted earlier, this finding may well be due to the fact that offenders sentenced by male judges were overrepresented in the sample used for the logistic regression when compared to the sample used for the cross tabulated analysis, which may have created the discrepancy. It may also be that there are differences in the way male and female judges sentence offenders. Surely, there are those who argue that women act differently than men (Gilligan, 1982).

Our other judicial characteristics, sentencing philosophy and the ethnicity of the justices, did not affect sentencing in a consistent manner in this model. White judges were not significantly more likely than nonwhites to impose jail terms (OR = .48, n.s.), nor were retribution-oriented judges more likely to incarcerate offenders than judges who followed other sentencing philosophies (OR = 2.6, n.s.). Once again, it appears that either the reduced sample size or the inclusion of other factors lessened the statistical importance of these extralegal factors in predicting the use of jail.

Length of hearing, one of our measures of cooperation with the court, was associated with the likelihood of jail. Offenders whose hearings were four or more minutes were 1.9 times as likely as offenders with intermediate length hearings and 3.8 times as likely as offenders with short hearings (a minute or less) to be incarcerated (OR = 1.9, p < .001). This finding may be a function of the arraignment process. One would expect the arraignments of those who are ultimately incarcerated to take longer than other arraignments because the judges read all the charges and prior convictions before accepting pleas and setting sentences; this process would presumably take longer if the offender faced multiple charges or had prior convictions. This does not, however, preclude other interpretations.

The question remains whether hearing length "causes" the ultimate sentence or if the sentence "causes" the length of the hearing. It would not be surprising to learn that when stakes are high, the courtroom actors take more time.

Our other measure of courtroom organization, the presence of defense counsel, was not associated with the judges' decisions to incarcerate.

CONCLUSION

Our analyses of the effects of legal, extralegal, and organizational variables on judicial sentencing indicate that, for the most part, sentencing in our sample was based on legal factors (e.g., prior record, number of charges, appearance in custody). The only extralegal factor that appeared to have a consistent effect on judges' likelihoods of using jail was offenders' fluency in English. Here, those who spoke languages other than English were more likely to be incarcerated. In the next chapter, we discuss the meaning of our findings within a larger context.

CHAPTER 6

THE PROCESS OF DOING JUSTICE: DISCUSSION AND CONCLUSIONS

The courts we observed processed relatively few traditional misdemeanors, such as assaults or thefts, and an almost microscopic percentage of the offenses involved clear harm to victims. Rather, much of the courts' time was taken up with victimless crimes; homeless addicts who were drunk or under the influence of some other drug, careless motorists driving on suspended licenses, or streetwalkers plying their trade on busy avenues.

As in other municipal courts, the judges dealt with heavy case loads by accepting a high rate of guilty pleas during hearings that lasted but a few minutes. On a few occasions, to speed matters along, small groups of unrelated defendants were together apprised of their rights, or, after accepting multiple individual pleas, the judges simultaneously sentenced small collections of violators to probation.

Few of the defendants we studied were represented by counsel and as a result plea bargains were routinely manufactured by prosecutors and the judges who made offers to the defendants during their arraignments. Often, these propositions included reducing misdemeanor charges to infractions or lowering fines in exchange for guilty pleas. The situation is far from ideal. It is hard to put aside the notion that in such circumstances defendants are not so subtly coerced into cooperation as judges lose their facade of impartiality and appear as allies of the prosecutor.

The Sanctions

Monetary fines were the most common punishment handed out by the judges. Almost half of the offenders paid for their misdeeds out of their wallets. On average, the financial levies were higher than those reported elsewhere (Feeley, 1979; Ragona & Ryan, 1983; Ryan, 1980–81), but this was probably due to the raised cost of living.[1]

Nearly a third (31%) of the offenders were sentenced by the judges to jail; however, the percentage of individuals who eventually were incarcerated was probably higher. Our sample included only defendants who agreed to their guilt at arraignment, and none of them incurred the additional penalties that are often associated with pleading not guilty (Eisenstein & Jacob, 1977; Mileski, 1971). We cannot estimate the incarceration rates for those who waded further into the changing tides of the justice system, but can presume that they would be higher than the rate we found for those who initially admitted guilt.

Although not mentioned by other researchers, we found that community service was regularly imposed on our defendants; nearly 10 percent of the offenders in our sample received some form of it. Its absence from other court research is undoubtedly due to the rise in the popularity of community service that occurred after most of the other studies' data were collected. For the most part, at the request of the offenders, the judges assigned the alternative punishment to replace fines.

The Judges

Overall, the judges who presided over the courts under study were similar to those described elsewhere.[2] The majority were middle-aged, white, and male. However, a substantial portion of the municipal court judges in the county were female; nearly a third (8 of 27) of the judges we interviewed were women. This may indicate that women in greater numbers are gaining access to the judicial field.

Women may bring with them values and ideologies that are different from their male brethren and transform sentencing norms. The results of our study with regard to this matter are unclear. Our most sophisticated analysis, however, indicated that women were less likely to send offenders to jail.[3]

THE DETERMINATION OF PENALTIES

The judges relied heavily on the legal factors of cases to reach their sentencing decisions. Prior records, multiple charges, and pretrial detention increased offenders' likelihood of incarceration. Extralegal offender characteristics rarely were associated with punishment decisions.[4] The only item that was associated with judges' choices to incarcerate offenders was proficiency in English. Defendants who did not speak English were more likely to be sent to jail. For the most part, these were Hispanics.

Items, other than the legal characteristics of the offenders' cases did seem to play some role in their chances for jail. Most glaring was the variation in sentencing between judges. In particular, a minority of judges who followed a retribution-oriented philosophy of punishment sentenced most offenders to jail.[5] But when leniency was granted by these heavy-handed judges, it was done unevenly and in a pattern that disadvantaged weaker defendants. When jail was likely, the judges selected for leniency those offenders whose ethnicity or gender matched their own.[6]

The bias noted by previous researchers may be the result of the sentencing practices of a few judges whose decision-making differs widely from their counterparts. Bias in favor of some groups, for example, may be manifest within a small subset of judges whose sentencing is so different from their colleagues that it causes all judges to appear tainted.

ORGANIZATIONAL VARIABLES

Characteristics of the courtroom process played a role in the sentencing of our sample of offenders. Those defendants who faced severe penalties, because of the charges against them and their prior records, were more likely to obtain counsel and plead not guilty. But those with attorneys who did plead guilty were more likely to be jailed, usually as part of a plea agreement.

Our second organizational variable, length of hearing also played a part in offenders' ultimate punishments. Those who took more of the courts' time were more likely to be jailed for these efforts, even when other variables were controlled. In fact, the longer an offender's hearing, the more inevitable incarceration became. Those who protest their innocence by presenting evidence in their favor or who do not allow themselves to be shuttled out of the courtroom without a "proper hearing" may receive harsh penalties to compensate for the annoyance they caused the courtroom work group.

Of course, the association between lengthy hearings and jail may simply be a case of mistaken antecedent; the seriousness of offenders' crimes and the eventual penalties associated with this criminality may cause courtroom work groups to spend more time on the cases. There were instances, however, where nonserious cases took extra time and resulted in incarceration for defendants; most notably for offenders who required translators.

DISCUSSION

What have we learned? We began this book by noting that criticisms of judges were not new. More than two hundred years ago, Cesare Beccaria, a classical theorist, criticized the criminal justice system of his day. Punishments, he argued, were irrational. Thieves, for example, might receive the death penalty. Given that this was the worst that might befall them, Beccaria wondered what incentive there was for thieves not to kill their victims. They could, he pointed out, avoid identification while adding nothing to the severity of their potential punishments. In addition, capital punishment was unevenly applied. The church might step in and grant clemency to certain offenders. More often, judges decided to lessen the penalties on their own, and were unlikely to convict or sentence harshly if they felt the punishments exceeded the severity of the offenders' crimes.

Beccaria attributed some of the uneven application of punishments to bias; powerful defendants were treated with favor by the courts while the powerless were sanctioned severely. In particular, when penalties were severe, he asserted, they were applied by judges only to the weak and disapproved. Heavy penalties, then, lead to unequal treatment.

Beccaria prescribed cures for the ills that plagued the criminal justice system. First, he urged that legislators, as representatives of the people, determine sentences. Offenders would then be able to weigh the costs and benefits of criminal behavior. The use of legislated penalties would also protect offenders from the continuing tyranny of judges who imposed sentences based on favoritism.

Next, Beccaria proposed that the severity of punishments be decreased. Penalties should be moderate to ensure that they will be applied in all cases. Severe legislated penalties often result in plea bargains that allow defendants to receive punishments more in line with their offenses. Lessening penalties may remove the need for such legal machinations. In addition, offenders would know the penalties they would incur for their criminal acts, which, from Beccaria's view, would allow for rational decision-making.

Much of what the municipal court justices told us and what we gleaned from our analyses of their sentencing practices support Beccaria's views. The judges decried and avoided penalties they believed to be too severe. Penalties for drug use were singled out for particular attention. The penalty for driving while intoxicated, the judges noted, was less than for being in public under the influence of drugs. They argued that the potential for harm from drunken drivers was greater than from drug addicts and punishments should reflect this. The judges particularly disliked harsh mandatory sentences and found ways to circumvent them. Jail sentences and fines, for example, were sometimes replaced with probation or community corrections such as counseling or public service. As Beccaria would have understood, some relatively powerless individuals in our sample, non-English speakers, were treated more harshly than their more powerful counterparts.

Beccaria would take great umbrage at the irrationality that characterized the courts under study. The varying sentencing philosophies by our judges resulted in uneven use of punishments. Judges who followed the retribution-oriented philosophy were more likely to incarcerate offenders. Defendants appearing before one judge might receive a lenient sentence, while those appearing before other judges might be sentenced more severely for the same offenses.

The defendants in our sample would have had great difficulty determining beforehand the judicial consequences of their criminal acts, and hence would be difficult to deter from future offenses. Their ultimate sentences depended more on individual biases and characteristics of the judges than on the amount of harm offenders caused (as evidenced by the lack of victims in most cases). This probably undermines the legitimacy of the courts. Individuals are unlikely to view as just a system that treats one person one way and another quite differently.

Beccaria's solutions to the problems highlighted in our study would be quite radical. Legislative setting of penalties, wholesale decriminalization of behaviors, and greatly reduced penalties would be but a few of his answers.

Many of Beccaria's suggestions would be difficult to implement. His recommendation that legislators set penalties, for example, does not consider offenders' varying levels of culpability. Some offenders play relatively minor roles in criminal acts, while others are major actors. It also seems unlikely that elected legislators will deem it politically wise to decriminalize behaviors or lessen penalties. The current favored policy to imprison for decades those convicted of three separate felonies is an example of the danger of allowing only legislated penalties to be applied.

We can, however, take Beccaria's advice to heart. His concern that the powerless are treated more harshly could be addressed through several means. Providing counsel for all defendants at the arraignment stage might increase the equality of treatment for defendants. In particular, bilingual attorneys for non-English speakers might reduce inequality. Non-English speakers, more so than others, may benefit from the presence of an ally from within the circle of the courtroom work group.[7]

Judges' discussions amongst themselves with respect to the purpose of punishment might also help achieve Beccaria's goal of equal and, therefore, predictable penalties. Judges, for example, might reach agreement on the use of alternative sanctions such as probation and community service and add consistency to their sentencing decisions.

CHANGES IN JUDICIAL COMPOSITION

Changes in the composition of judges is the factor that will most likely alter punishment for defendants. An increase in the percentage of judges who hold retribution as the primary purpose of punishment will most likely result in some bias. Our results indicate that such individuals jail offenders at a high rate (62% compared to 23% for other punishment philosophies). They choose for leniency those individuals who are most like themselves. More lenient judges, who held punishment philosophies other than retribution, did not appear to favor one group over another.

The judiciary is changing. Most notable are the increasing numbers of female and minority judges. These groups may have different values and philosophies than the traditional white, middle-class, male justice and alter the general portrait of punishment.

The entrance of large numbers of women into the judiciary is a phenomenon of the last twenty-five years (Berkson, 1982). As with most areas of the workplace, women were denied access to the legal bar based on age-old divisions of labor and discrimination. As late as 1869, Illinois denied "Mrs." Myra Bradwell admission to the bar. A member of the U.S. Supreme Court, in a concurring opinion upholding the state's decision, reflected the general mores of the male-dominated society:

> [C]ivil law, as well as nature herself, has always recognized a wide difference in the respective spheres and destinies of man and woman. Man is, or should be, woman's protector and defender. The natural and proper timidity and delicacy which belongs to the female sex evidently fits it for many of the occupations of civil life. The constitution of the family organization, which is founded in the divine ordinance, as well as in the nature of things, indicates the domestic sphere as that which properly belongs to the domain and functions of womanhood. (*Bradwell v. Illinois*, 1872, p. 141)

There was a smattering of women judges in the late 1800s and by 1930 twelve states had, at one time, seated at least one female judge (Berkson, 1982). The number of women judges increased after the rise of the women's movement around 1970. That year, women comprised about 5 percent of the judiciary (U.S. Bureau of the Census, 1973). Two decades later their percentage had increased more than fourfold to 23 percent (U.S. Bureau of the Census, 1992). The expanded numbers of women admitted to law schools guarantees that women will continue to comprise a growing percentage of justices.

The increasing number of women entering the legal field as both judges and attorneys may alter the philosophy and practice of law. The prestige of the legal profession has been in public decline for some time, most likely due to the public's perception of lawyers as "greedy bastards." "What do you call a bus load of lawyers at the bottom of a lake?" So goes the start of hundreds of attorney jokes that regularly appear on the information superhighway. "A good start," is the cynical punch line.

Whether women will be able to change the profession's poor image remains to be seen. There are, however, those whose writings suggest that women in general have different ways of doing and thinking about things. Carol Gilligan (1982) is probably the most often cited for her assertion that women conceptualize moral questions as problems of care involving empathy and compassion, while men see such problems as matters of rights. Based on Gilligan's work one would expect women who enter the legal field to bring with them a nurturing, collaborative, cooperative spirit that mediates the aggressiveness and self-interest that motivates men.

Research on women judges has shown some differences between them and their male counterparts. Demographically, they are younger and more likely to have attended private law schools (Carbon, Houlden, & Berkson, 1982), matters most likely associated with women's recent entry into judicial positions.

Women also appear to have different philosophies regarding the law. Women appellate court judges, for example, in one study were more likely to support claimants in employment discrimination cases and defendants in search and seizure matters (Davis, Haire, & Songer, 1993). A survey of state and federal women judges reported that they felt female justices brought "unique perspectives" to the bench and were "more sensitive" then male judges to claimants alleging sexual discrimination (Martin, 1993).

Not all women judges speak in the "different voice" that Gilligan (1982) discussed. All judges are, in part, reflective of those who appoint them. In particular, federal judges' share some norms with the presidents who appoint them. Women judges appointed by reform-minded Jimmy Carter, on the one hand, were more likely than Carter's male appointments to assume primary responsibility for their households, and experience conflict between their judgeships and parental roles. The majority reported overcoming sexual discrimination obstacles on the path to their legal careers (Martin, 1990). On the other hand, an analysis of opinions by Supreme Court Justice Sandra Day O'Connor, a Ronald Reagan appointee, noted that she does not "appear to 'speak in a different voice'" (Davis, 1993, p. 139). It is unlikely that Carter would have nominated Sandra Day O'Connor and Reagan would not have nominated Carter's female appointments, including Ruth Bader Ginsburg, the most recent female addition to the U.S. Supreme Court.

Some women judges may not exercise their voice because it would be politically unwise to abandon their status as "neutral decision-makers" in a profession that is dominated by men (Davis, Haire, & Songer, 1993). As more women enter the field, however, they may be more willing to speak in their own distinctive voice.

In our study of judges, we found support for Gilligan's (1982) suggestion that there are differences between men and women. For example, the female judges did mention items connected with nurturing or helping others. Indicative are the comments of one of them, who said she was attracted to the municipal courts because she could help others:

> The reason why I like Muni Court is that . . . you have a greater opportunity to engage in treatment and reformation. You're usually seeing people at an earlier stage in their criminal career, before anything really nasty and horrible has happened, so that you can pull them out of the downwards spiral that they often get into. . . . In Muni Court, you have a hope of making a difference out of somebody's life.

Victims were particularly important to the female judges. More than half (5 of 8) mentioned victims as playing a role in their sentencing, compared to less than a third (6 of 19) of the male judges. One female judge, for example, noted that concern for victims affected the severity of her sentences. "Violent crimes," she told us, "generally warrant incarceration for protection of the victims, and not only victims of that crime, [but] potential victims who may testify."

Male judges, on the other hand, were more likely to focus on the crime and the offender when deciding sentences. Illustrative are the comments of the following male judge:

> The factors that go into [the sentencing of offenders] are primarily their background, their age, the nature of the offence, any violence involved . . . that sort of thing. Was it well planned, well thought out? Did they act alone? Did they act with somebody else?

The results of our study with respect to judicial gender and sentencing do not provide a clear picture of differences, but do provide an impressionistic view. The female judges, at first glance, were more likely to sentence repeat offenders to jail, but this difference disappeared when we excluded the two outlier judges who incarcerated nearly all the offenders who were unfortunate enough to appear before them. When we controlled for other variables in our multivariate analysis, men were more likely than their female associates to jail offenders.

Perhaps of greater interest was our result indicating that each gender favored its own. Male judges were more likely to jail female offenders and female judges were more likely to incarcerate males. This finding continued to exist when we controlled for offense severity and prior record. Eliminating from the analysis the two outlier judges did not alter the result.[8]

Our results intimate that the genders' approach to sentencing may differ. As more women enter the judiciary, then, punishment patterns may be altered.

Minority Judges

Minority judges, like women judges, may "inject new perspectives into the law" (Martin, 1993, p. 173). Minorities also are increasing in number within the judiciary; their rise parallels that of women. In 1970, they comprised less than 3 percent of the total number of judges (U.S. Bureau of the Census, 1973). By 1990, their percentage had increased slightly more than fourfold to 12 percent (U.S. Bureau of the Census, 1992).

The race of justices has long been perceived as important by researchers, although rarely stated. Sellin, in his seminal 1928 work certainly must have considered that the bias he was reporting was an outgrowth of white justices sentencing black defendants (see Chapter 2 for a discussion of judicial race and sentencing studies).

Our study provides scant information on sentencing by minority judges. We collected arraignment data on only two of their number. Our analyses indicate, however, that white and minority judges may, in some instances, sentence equally the offenders before them. While white judges were significantly more likely than minority judges to use jail, this difference disappeared when we excluded the two outlier judges. In addition, our multivariate analysis, which controlled for legal and extralegal factors, failed to reveal any differences between the punishments handed out by white and minority judges. The information suggests that, for the most part, white and minority justices similarly sentence defendants, as both groups rely on legal factors in making such decisions.

Cumulative Bias

Although judges can certainly play a role in discrimination against ethnic minorities and other less powerful groups, our results combined with those of others strongly indicate that such bias is not overly prevalent and can be further diminished by some fairly easy means (see our suggestions earlier in this chapter). This is not to intimate that bias by judges be ignored. Only that the discrimination that does occur is not institutionalized within the judiciary, but rather is the result of the actions of a few judges.

That judges appear to rely for the most part on legal matters in their sentencing decisions should not be considered a wholesale affirmation for the criminal justice system. The culture of defendants in our study did play a role in their punishments. Such bias probably also exists at other levels of the system. It is important to recognize that bias may be a cumulative product resulting from multiple contacts with criminal justice personnel, including police, prosecutors, and probation personnel whose decisions are a lot less public than are judges' (Lizotte, 1978; Pepinsky & Jesilow, 1984; Uhlman 1977; 1979).

One often overlooked source of discrimination is the state and federal legislature. It is here that institutionalized bias can begin. For example, laws that mandate more severe penalties for possession of "crack" cocaine than for powder cocaine are based, at least in part, on the fact that innercity blacks are more likely to be caught with crack while powder cocaine is the drug of choice for upper-class white youth (Mann, 1995).

Some researchers have found that mandatory sentencing criteria may be subtly "tainted" for or against whites (Lemert & Rosberg, 1948; Petersilia & Turner, 1985).

Cumulative bias also may be contributed to by the status of victims and offenders. Which individuals get arrested, prosecuted, and convicted may have a lot to do with the socioeconomic status of their victims. Intraracial minority offenses may not be punished harshly because such crimes are not a threat to white elites (Myers, 1987; Myers & Talarico, 1988). Hence, misdeeds in poor neighborhoods are sometimes ignored by the system. A respected sociologist (Black, 1980, pp. 9–10), for example, noted that domestic disputes involving minority victims receive less police attention.

White-collar crimes committed against indigents may generate even less interest from the system. In general, society does not appear that concerned with what happens to rich, white defendants who victimize the poor via illegal practices (such as bank decisions not to lend to those in certain neighborhoods, usually low-income areas).

Bias may depend more on socioeconomic status than race. The fact that prosecutors agreed not to seek the death penalty for O.J. Simpson, for example, was probably more a function of his status in society than his race. For other defendants, wealth may mean the ability to secure adequate counsel or post bail (Lizotte, 1978; Uhlman 1977; 1979). A contribution to cumulative bias may result for those who are unable to obtain these essentials.

Criminal justice personnel other than judges may decide how long offenders stay in prison. Prosecutors, because of their power to bring charges against defendants, decide whether offenders will face mandatory terms of incarceration. Parole boards and wardens (through good-time policies) make release decisions for inmates in some jurisdictions. Juries decide sentences in most capital cases and for some other offenses.[9] These decisions, as all others in the criminal justice system, may be influenced by bias based on race, culture, and other factors. Since they are exposed to less public scrutiny, however, decisions by agents other than judges may be more invidious and difficult to isolate.

In our study, the legal mandate that justices jail individuals convicted of certain offenses led to overfilled jails and transferred discretion for release dates to the county sheriff. While we do not have information on which defendants were released through this pressure valve, we could conjecture that extralegal factors such as attitude played some role in the decisions.

CONCLUSION

We began this study with the belief that bias exists in sentencing. We felt, however, that this bias was not simply the product of a single factor, such as the race of a defendant, but that it was an outcome of the interaction between complex human beings and courtroom processes.

During interviews, the judges reported that, for the most part, they attempt to "do justice" in their fashioning of sentences. "Doing justice" means the use of discretion to fit punishments to individual circumstances. They told us they use legal variables such as offense severity and prior record when determining penalties and that extralegal factors rarely affect these decisions, facts supported by our analyses of their sentencing. They argued that discretion was necessary for them to achieve their goals and they disliked forces such as mandatory sentences and jail overcrowding that curtailed their freedom to implement penalties of their choosing. Discretion, however, inevitably leads to unequal treatment. In general, we found that individual judicial characteristics, rather than extralegal offender demographics, were associated with unequal treatment. In particular, the varying ideologies of the judges resulted in disparate penalties for similar offenses.

Eliminating justices' use of discretion and the bias that naturally accompanies it, however, would simply shift it to other actors in the system, such as police or prosecutors. Such circumstances would be far from desirable since their actions are a lot less public than judges.

We know that bias exists, not only with judges, but at all levels of the criminal justice system. The task is to seek to understand when and why it takes place. Rather than focusing on determining if bias exists, researchers should attempt to fathom its causes and make suggestions to lessen its impact on victims and offenders.

NOTES

CHAPTER 1

1. In some jurisdictions, including California, municipal court judges can hear some felonies.

2. To state that misdemeanors are less serious than felonies does not adequately reflect the fact that many misdemeanors may be "more serious" in terms of harm or affect on the community. In some states (including California), it is the sentence given that determines the classification of certain crimes (often referred to as "wobblers") as felonies or misdemeanors; only after the sentence has been pronounced, can the crime be correctly categorized. Further, crimes that are misdemeanors in one state may be felonies in another; sometimes, this irregular classification occurs between counties in the same state. Misdemeanors, then, are less serious only in terms of the sanctions that judges may apply.

3. The public became aware of such practices during the O.J. Simpson murder case as first one attorney, then another were hired for their specialized expertise in each stage of the judicial process.

CHAPTER 2

1. This decision was a civil judgment concerning "separate, but equal" policies and did not specifically address sentencing differences. It does, however, illustrate the institutionalized inequity of the time.

2. These eleven crimes were burglary, armed robbery, simple larceny, assault and battery, disturbing the peace, accosting and

soliciting, common prostitution, sex crimes, offenses against the state drug laws, violations of state prohibition codes, and offenses involving embezzling, forgery, uttering, or publishing.

3. We did not compute differences for manslaughter and negligent homicide because the number of convictions exceeded the number of arrests.

4. Judges' instructions to juries are not the only potential source of bias that leads to disparate sentencing by juries (Fukurai, Butler, & Krooth, 1993).

5. Six years after the publication of Sellin's work, Roscoe Martin (1934) concurred with Sellin's finding that race of defendant impacted severity of sentence and found that blacks received longer sentences than whites. Martin considered the effects of race, occupation, age, and sex on punishments handed out to 927 Texas offenders in 1930. Since Martin's original paper could not be found, the results reported here are based on John Hagan's (1974) review of the literature. Like Sellin, Martin did not include tests of significance; unlike his predecessor, however, he failed to control for any legal variables such as offense type. Martin, then, represents both a move forward and a move backward in methodological terms. While he introduced other extralegal factors for future researchers to consider, his research was less sophisticated than Sellin's due to his lack of legal controls.

6. Tests of significance allow the researchers to state that results are not apt to be due to coincidence. Most research prior to 1950 did not determine the likelihood of findings being attributable to fluke, leaving readers to peruse the tables and statistics and speculate for themselves whether or not the findings were statistically valid.

7. This additional statistic (the contingency coefficient of association) allows readers to judge how much variance is explained by the variables.

8. Unlike many jurisdictions, juries in Texas can sentence in both misdemeanor and felony cases where the defendant has pleaded guilty. Defendants choose between being sentenced by the judge or jury. When a defendant pleads guilty to a jury, the jury hears the case and is then directed by the judge to "find" the defendant guilty. After "finding" the defendant guilty, the jury proceeds with the penalty phase of the case (personal communication with El Paso (Texas) court coordinator M. Bailey, 1993).

9. By collecting data for inmates in prison, Bullock (1961) effectively eliminated two potentially important types of defendants whose inclusion might have altered his results: those sentenced to death and those assigned to chain gangs. Offenders sentenced to death were excluded by Bullock because he omitted inmates awaiting execution and could not gather data for those already executed. It is possible that this affected his unexpected finding that black murderers were sentenced more leniently than white murderers. Garfinkel's (1949) work on offender-victim dyads suggests that all murders are not viewed the same by sentencing agents. If blacks were sentenced to death for murders of whites, but given short sentences for murders of other blacks, it is likely that only blacks who killed other blacks were included in Bullock's study. And if whites are more likely than nonwhites to have their death sentences commuted (e.g., Bedau, 1964, p. 20), it is possible that a number of white murderers had their sentences changed to life imprisonment while black murderers were executed, making them unavailable for study. Similarly, chain gang members would not be included in Bullock's study. Jesse Steiner and Roy Brown (1927, pp. 136–37, as cited in Sellin, 1928) noted that blacks were more likely to be sentenced to chain gangs while whites convicted of the same offenses would be sent to prison. Offenders sentenced to chain gangs would not be represented in Bullock's prison sample, which could easily bias his findings.

10. For minor property offenses, defendants were sentenced less harshly if they pleaded guilty. Green suggested that this finding may be attributed more to the defendants' willingness to make restitution to the victim than to the actual guilty plea.

11. There is no evidence to support the concept that whites are more likely than blacks to be skid row inhabitants. The differences noted by Mileski between black and white offenders arrested for being drunk in public might have been the result of police activities. Officers may have chosen to handle rowdy, young, employed, intoxicated whites in a manner other than arresting them.

12. It may well be that the number of motions indicates that the cases were not similar to begin with. Defendants facing long sentences may have made every possible motion in order to better their chances of acquittal or appeal.

13. Defendant race was unimportant in Chicago, but according to the authors, may have influenced decisions to imprison in Baltimore and Detroit.

14. The independent variables included: identity of the courtroom, disposition stage, disposition mode, strength of the evidence, characteristics of the defendant, and type of offense.

15. Of interest, Eisenstein and Jacob (1977, p. 189, footnote 4) used a 1975 version of SPSS (Statistical Program for the Social Sciences) for their computations, thus indicating that computer resources were available for those completing research in the social sciences.

16. The felonies examined included: second-degree murder, voluntary manslaughter, involuntary manslaughter, forcible rape, statutory rape, aggravated assault, armed robbery, unarmed robbery, burglary, larceny, receiving stolen property, auto theft, embezzlement, forgery, drug offenses, escape, and arson. These crimes were selected because they were the only offenses for which at least twenty offenders were convicted. First-degree murder was excluded because of the lack of variation; murders in the first degree were punished almost exclusively with life imprisonment or death.

17. Florida was the only state for which demographic data and prior records were available to the researchers.

18. Stepwise models rank independent variables based on the amount of variance they account for in the dependant variable.

19. Race, for example, explained less than 2 percent of the variance for twelve of thirteen Florida offenses. For the one exception, second degree murder, race was the most important predictor of sentence length and explained 7 percent of the variance.

20. Path analysis is a multivariate technique that allows researchers to calculate the exact amount of influence on the dependent variable due to any single "path" (either an independent variable that is directly related to the dependent variable or a series of independent variables that act together to influence the dependent variable).

21. The independent variables fell into three categories: (1) legal (prior arrests, offense seriousness, and amount of evidence); (2) extralegal (race, socioeconomic status, and ability to post bail); and, (3) organizational (bail amount, and defense attorney's degree of success).

22. Race and occupation were presented together as exogenous variables.

23. Findings by others support Lizotte. Researchers on the Manhattan Bail Project found that defendants held in custody before trial

were more likely to be convicted than those who were free before their trials (Ares, Rankin, & Sturz, 1963).

24. Although the difference was statistically significant, blacks were only 4 percent more likely than whites to be convicted.

25. Welch and associates (1984) regressed their two dependent variables (whether the defendant was sent to prison and sentence severity) on the eleven measures of prior record, while controlling for type of offense. They did this for blacks, then for whites.

26. The terms "Hispanics" and "Chicanos" are both used by Zatz.

27. The independent variables included area inequality measures (e.g., percent black and the difference between white and black mean income in each county), legal variables (e.g., offense seriousness and prior record), extralegal characteristics of offenders (e.g., race and age), and control variables (e.g., index crime rate and percentage of crimes involving weapons).

28. Income inequality is "indicated by county income standard deviation based on 1979 Census family income data" (Myers, 1987, p. 750). Those areas with high variance (i.e., areas with large income differences between citizens) have greater income inequality.

29. In addition to race of judge and defendant, Spohn examined the effects of type of offense, number of instant offenses, prior record, weapon use, injury to victim, whether the victim was a stranger, type of attorney, type of plea, pretrial detention, and defendant age and gender on sentence severity (whether or not the offender was sent to prison and the sentence length).

30. To determine if black and white judges sentenced black and white offenders differently, Spohn (1990) ran separate regressions to test for differences between judges when sentencing those of their own race versus others. The regressions were run on four separate samples: (1) black judge/black offender, (2) black judge/white offender, (3) white judge/white offender, and (4) white judge/black offender.

CHAPTER 3

1. One of the interviewed subjects was a municipal court commissioner hearing misdemeanor criminal cases and another subject

was a municipal court commissioner hearing minor traffic cases, such as speeding or making an illegal turn. Any information that might specifically identify a judge or the county has been excluded to protect their anonymity.

2. We sent letters to all of the lower court judges sitting in the county under study asking if we could interview them for this project. During follow-up phone calls made to their chambers, we assured them that we would keep their identities and words confidential and explained the study in further detail. If the judges wished to take part, we scheduled an interview.

3. In addition to individualized questions, the judges were asked how they became interested in becoming a judge, what they saw as their role in the criminal justice system, what factors they felt were most important in sentencing, the purposes they had in mind when deciding punishments, and how they felt about community service sentences, mandatory penalties, and their level of discretion.

4. Some judges mentioned more than one item.

5. The judges' statements regarding drug laws highlight their belief that the control of drug use would be better handled outside the criminal justice system.

6. California Penal Code Section 1385 allows justices to dismiss charges.

7. It is difficult to believe that someone might actually freeze to death in the county under study. The temperature, except in the few higher elevations which are sparsely populated, rarely drops below freezing.

8. To further expand their discretion, some of the judges converted the fines before the addition of the penalty assessment (the penalty assessment, a legislated fee paid in addition to the fine, was 170 percent of the amount of the fine). This creative judicial arithmetic served to reduce the number of hours of community service a given defendant would be asked to perform. To illustrate this process, consider the mandatory drunk driving fine of $390. After the addition of the penalty assessment, however, the fine increased to over $1,000. By converting the fine to community service before considering the penalty assessment, approximately fourteen fewer days of service were required.

9. Because the vast majority of judges (23 of 27) utilized more than one sentencing philosophy as they attempted to fashion penalties to fit offenders, the number of judges supporting each philosophy does not add up to twenty-seven.

Chapter 4

1. We tried to collect the defendant's name and demographic information (i.e., ethnicity, gender, physical soundness, fluency in English, number of hours employed, style of dress, and age), presence and type of defense counsel, whether the defendant was in custody, who participated in the hearing (e.g., defendant, judge, prosecutor, defense attorney, victim, lay or expert witness, or others), nature of communication between the judge and defendant, judge's identity, date and type of hearing, number of continuances, date of original hearing, quality of evidence presented, prior record, nature of the charges, sentence, and duration of the hearing.

2. Research indicates that those represented by attorneys are more likely to plead guilty (e.g., Blumberg, 1967; Eisenstein & Jacob, 1977; Nardulli, 1978). Organizational theorists argue that this represents attorneys' attempts to cooperate with other members of the courtroom work group.

3. It is important to note that the sentences in our sample resulted from "fast" guilty pleas; fast guilty pleas are those that are entered immediately while "slow" guilty pleas are entered some time after the initial appearance (Meeker & Pontell, 1985). Since fast guilty pleas are less adversarial than slow guilty pleas, sentences resulting from the two may differ in terms of severity.

4. These minor traffic charges were arraigned in municipal court instead of traffic court because they were add-on charges to other, more serious, offenses. In many cases, for example, individuals driving on suspended licenses were detected through minor traffic violations. This process also applies for fix-it tickets and seat belt violations.

5. "Fix-it" tickets mandate repair of some defective automobile part. Some of the tickets, for example, required the defendants to repair damaged windshields or fix broken lights.

6. It is not uncommon to release minor offenders with orders to report to the jail on a certain date to serve their sentence. In addition

to those who choose to serve their terms on weekends, some defendants often prefer to delay their sentences so they can arrange their personal lives and notify their places of employment. Offenders given this option, however, do not always report to serve their sentence.

7. A problem associated with having the judges announce defendants' prior records was that the judges may have been sensitized to the presence of a given defendant's prior record by making these statements. This may have affected the ultimate sentences. In crowded courtrooms, the judges may have been more likely to impose harsh sanctions on those with publicly announced records to increase the general deterrent value. The judges may also have wanted to appear as though they gave harsher sentences because of defendants' prior convictions. Second, some defendants may have decided to change their pleas only because their records were publicly announced. Although these problems may not have altered our findings in any significant way, they may further limit the representativeness of our sample.

8. As discussed earlier, we do not know the outcome of cases in which individuals entered pleas of "not guilty."

9. This relationship held for all categories. For example, 27 percent of first-time offenders who faced less than a year in jail pleaded not guilty compared to 39 percent of their counterparts who faced more time (phi = .15, p < .01), while 59 percent of individuals charged with a single serious offense (one that carried a possible maximum penalty of a year in jail) pled not guilty.

10. According to a Bureau of Justice Statistics publication, 51 percent of 1991 and 1992 adult jail inmates were "unconvicted" (Beck, Bonczar, & Gilliard, 1993). These figures, however, include individuals on trial or awaiting arraignment or trial for felonies as well as misdemeanors.

11. In-custody defendants are often sentenced to "time served" in exchange for admissions of culpability. The jail sentences assigned to offenders in our sample, however, were always periods in excess of the day or two defendants had spent in jail awaiting their arraignments.

12. Presence and type of defense counsel was noted by the courtroom observers. Over 90 percent (93%) of the defendants in our sample appeared without representation (n = 1467). Five percent were represented by public defenders (n = 86). Two percent were represented by private attorneys (n = 25). Two defendants were rep-

resented by attorneys, but the observers could not determine whether they were private attorneys or public defenders. We were unable to determine whether twenty defendants had legal counsel.

13. Thirteen percent of those who could be jailed for one year or more had attorneys compared to only 4 percent of those who faced less time (phi = .15, p < .0001); 10 percent of repeat offenders had attorneys compared to only 1 percent of those without prior convictions (phi = .16, p < .0001); 5 percent of repeat offenders facing less than one year in jail had defense counsel compared to none of their counterparts without records (phi = .14, p < .001); 17 percent of repeat offenders facing a year or more in jail had attorneys compared to only 4 percent of first-time offenders confronting serious charges (phi = .15, p < .01).

14. Our finding that those with attorneys were less likely to plead guilty makes intuitive sense since the presence of counsel was correlated with offense severity, a factor we already determined to be associated with lower rates of guilty pleas.

15. The finding was significant when we controlled for offense severity (defendants facing less than one year in jail: phi = .09, p < .001; those facing more time: phi = .11, p < .05), but was not significant for repeat offenders (phi = .07, p = .07).

16. The guilty plea rates for non-English speakers may, in fact, have been deflated because the judges sometimes entered not guilty pleas for non-English speakers to give the court time to find translators.

17. When we factored in offense severity and prior record, the relationships remained; 74 percent of English-speaking defendants who faced less than a year in jail pleaded guilty compared to 81 percent of non-English speakers (phi = .06, p < .05). In addition, 72 percent of English speaking repeat offenders who faced less than a year in jail entered pleas of guilty compared to 89 percent of their non-English speaking counterparts (phi = .18, p < .01).

18. For defendants who sent attorneys to represent them in absentia, gender was recorded based on name or gender-referencing language used by members of the courtroom work group (e.g., "Where is he?").

19. Males admitted guilt in 70 percent of their cases versus 74 percent for women (phi = .03, n.s.). No significant differences emerged when we controlled for offense severity and prior record.

20. When we controlled for offense severity, the relationship held; 91 percent of offenders charged with court related offenses and facing less than one year in jail pleaded guilty compared to 71 percent of their counterparts who were not arraigned on court related charges (phi = .19, p < .001). For those facing more than one year in jail, 73 percent of offenders charged with court related offenses and 56 percent of those arraigned on other charges pleaded guilty (phi = .17, p < .001). When we added prior record to the model, however, the relationship held but was significant for only repeat offenders who faced less than a year in jail; 93 percent of such offenders pleaded guilty if they faced court related charges compared to only 63 percent who faced other charges (phi = .35, p < .0001).

21. Logistic regression allows multiple independent variables to be regressed on a dichotomous dependent variable. Additionally, when the assumption that the dependant variable is normally distributed is violated, logistic regression produces better estimates than would ordinary least squares (OLS) regression.

22. We ran the equation using Hispanics and blacks versus whites as well Hispanics versus whites. Neither ethnicity substitution changed the results much. No variables changed their "significancy" (i.e., all insignificant factors remained insignificant and all significant factors remained significant). Further, the parameters (odds ratios) changed by less than .2 for those that changed at all.

Chapter 5

1. The exact percent was 47 percent (n = 531).

2. Sixty-six offenders were able to substitute community service for a fine.

3. If offenders complete diversion programs, the charges against them will be dropped. One judge explained the concept of diversion: "If [offenders] successfully complete the program as ordered and they provide proof of completion afterwards, those charges will be dismissed. If they don't complete the program, . . . the criminal charges will be reinstated and they will be prosecuted on the offense."

4. Very few (1%, n = 10) of the misdemeanants in our study were probationed as their sole penalty; the vast majority of probationers received other penalties in addition to their term of supervi-

sion. In all, nearly a quarter of our offenders were placed on probation (24%, n = 271).

5. See chapter four for an explanation of how we computed maximum possible sentences.

6. Cross tabulations were used to make comparisons. We computed phi for 2 × 2 tables and Cramer's V for larger tables.

7. When seriousness of offense was controlled, the number of charges did not significantly affect the sentences for offenders facing less than one year in jail (phi = .02, n.s.). When offense severity and prior record were considered in addition to the number of charges, the number of charges significantly affected only repeat offenders who faced one year or more in jail. For these offenders, the more charges one faced, the higher one's likelihood of incarceration; 33 percent of such offenders who faced one charge were incarcerated compared with 59 percent of those who faced two charges and 78 percent of those who faced three or more charges (phi = .23, p < .05). It appears at first examination that the number of charges may be an influential factor in cases involving offenders who have visited the system before and whose criminality is more serious. An alternate explanation, however, may center on the fact that each additional charge often represents additional exposure to jail time. The number of charges may be very important for those offenders who accumulate so many charges that their possible maximum sentences are very long (e.g., 3 years or more). We were, however, unable to detect if this was the case, since only 3 percent of the sixteen hundred defendants faced three or more charges and the majority of these pleaded "not guilty" and were therefore not included in our analyses of judicial decisions.

8. Prior record affected the likelihood of jail for both those who faced a year or more in jail (phi = .42, p < .0001) and offenders who could be sanctioned less severely (phi = .40, p < .0001). It is important to remind the reader that we were unable to obtain information on prior criminal convictions for a portion of the sample. Our analyses which include "prior record," therefore, have fewer cases.

9. Thirty-seven percent of repeat offenders who faced less than one year actually were sentenced to jail compared to jail sentences for only 2 percent of first-time offenders in the same category.

10. It is not always clear, however, whether appearance in custody is a legal or extralegal attribute. Pretrial detention may be due to

offense seriousness, risk of flight, or socioeconomic status of defendants (i.e., financial inability to make bail).

We were concerned whether in-custody status was a legal or extralegal variable. Pretrial detention may act as a legal variable for some offenders (e.g., those charged with violent offenses whose bail was set very high or denied), but an extralegal one for others (e.g., those who could not afford to pay even minimal bonds). Treating as a legal variable something which is actually based on socioeconomic status would be incorrect.

Eighty percent of the defendants in our sample were not in custody at their arraignments (1,267 not in custody; 328 in custody). Individuals whose possible maximum sentences were one year or more were more likely to appear in custody at their arraignments; 43 percent of those who faced incarceration for one year or more were detained compared with only 10 percent of those who could be jailed for less time (phi = .39, p < .0001). Moreover, individuals who had prior records were more likely to be detained prior to arraignment than first-time offenders who faced similar sentences; 50 percent of repeat offenders versus 13 percent of first-timers (phi = .40, p < .0001).

It appears that being in custody at one's arraignment is associated with the severity of crimes the defendant committed and his or her prior record. There is one caveat to this finding. Some offenses that result in-custody status, in particular those that are court related, may be based on socioeconomic conditions. On the one hand, failure to appear for a scheduled court hearing or complete community service or attend mandatory counseling or classes may be due to economic factors. Offenders may have jobs that do not allow time off to attend to court-related business or they may be unable to afford a day off without wages. On the other hand, detention before trial for court-related offenses may represent the court's legitimate concerns that defendants may not appear for hearings. These individuals have already failed at least once in this regard.

We asked a county public defender which types of offenders are held in custody. She told us that while the police have "total discretion" on whether to release defendants without bail (release on own recognizance), court-related charges are treated by criminal justice personnel as probation violations. As such, these defendants should be much more likely to be detained before their arraignments.

To determine whether those charged with court-related offenses were more likely to be detained before their arraignments, we compared defendants' custody status with the types of charges they faced (court-related versus all other charges). We found that those who faced court-related charges were much more likely than those who faced other charges to be held in custody before their arraignments; 44 percent of those charged with court-related offenses were detained before arraignment compared with only 8 percent of those who faced other charges (phi = .43, p < .0001).

The dilemma for us is whether those charged with court-related offenses are more likely in custody because their behavior is similar to probation violations (as suggested by the public defender) or whether they are being detained as a result of socioeconomic reasons. Defendants in custody for court-related charges are a sizable portion of all in-custody cases (77%, n = 252) and may weaken our finding that detainment before trial is a legal variable.

To determine which of our variables were most associated with pretrial detention, we conducted a logistic regression analysis. We considered those factors that could possibly be associated with detention before trial. These included legal variables (i.e., offense severity, prior record, number of charges) and extralegal characteristics of the defendant (i.e., ethnicity, fluency in English, and gender).

Before reporting on the results, it is important to note some limitations. First, as this study focused on judicial sentencing, we failed to collect some information on defendants that might be associated with pretrial detention, such as employment status. Second, the at liberty defendants in our sample may not be representative of all defendants who are released before trial; we were able to collect data for all offenders who appeared in custody, but a percentage of those at liberty before arraignment may never appear for their hearings.

The results of the logistic regression analysis are shown in Table 5.1. As expected, prior record had a strong affect on defendants' likelihood of detention before their arraignments. Repeat offenders were more than eight times as likely as first-time offenders to appear in custody (OR = 8.4, p < .0001), controlling for other variables. Another anticipated finding was that offense severity affected the likelihood of detention before trial. Those who faced one year or more in jail were more than four times as likely than those who faced less time to be detained before their arraignments (OR = 4.1, p < .0001). Whether defendants faced any court-related charges also significantly affected their likelihoods of pretrial detention. Those who were charged with court related offenses were nearly three times as likely as other defendants to be detained before trial (OR = 2.8, p < .001).

TABLE 5.1
Logistic Regression Analysis Predicting Pretrial Detention

Variable	β	SE	df	Prob.	Odds ratio
facing year or more	1.419	.316	1	.000	4.132
prior record	2.123	.501	1	.000	8.360
white offender	−.331	.279	1	.235	.718
fluent in English	−.192	.314	1	.542	.826
male offender	.475	.409	1	.246	1.608
court related charges	1.026	.312	1	.001	2.790
number of charges	.163	.133	1	.222	1.177
constant	−4.841	.788	1	.000	

Summary statistics	χ^2	df	Prob.
−2 log likelihood	465.299	657	1.000
Model χ^2	165.579	7	.000
Improvement	165.579	7	.000
Goodness of fit	666.344	657	.392

Note: Percentage of correct dependent variable classification by model is 83.61 percent.

None of our extra-legal variables (race, fluency in English, gender) significantly affected whether defendants were held in custody before their arraignments. At this important stage in the criminal court process, extralegal offender characteristics did not appear to be related to pretrial detention. At least for our sample, it appears that legal variables are the determinants of whether defendants appear in-custody. As such, we treat pretrial detention as a legal factor and in the following section analyze its association with judicial sentencing.

11. Our finding that prearraignment detention affected sentencing held when we controlled for offense severity. When we factored in prior record, in-custody status significantly affected the sentences imposed on repeat offenders. Ninety percent of in-custody repeat offenders facing serious charges were incarcerated compared to 41 percent of their at-liberty counterparts (phi = .52, p < .0001); 84 percent of repeat offenders who appeared in-custody facing less serious charges were incarcerated compared to 30 percent of similar offenders who were free before arraignment (phi = .37, p < .0001). We also wanted to determine for first-time offenders the associa-

tion between a jail sentence and appearing in-custody. Only ten such offenders were incarcerated; although in-custody first-time offenders facing less than a year in jail were significantly more likely to be jailed (phi = .34, p < .0001). Custody status, however, did not significantly impact the likelihood of jail for first-time offenders facing serious charges. These results, however, are based on very small numbers.

12. Half of whites who faced possible maximum sentences of one year or more (our measure of offenders' crime severity) were sent to jail compared with 64 percent of their nonwhite counterparts (phi = .14, p < .01). Similarly, 16 percent of whites facing less than one year in jail were incarcerated, while 22 percent of nonwhites in the same category received jail (phi = .08, p < .05).

13. For offenses where the possible maximum penalty was less than one year, about 20 percent of individuals from any group went to jail (whites = 16%, blacks = 21%, Hispanics = 23%—not a statistically significant difference).

14. Marjorie Zatz (1985) suggested that Hispanics should be analyzed separately from blacks because they are a distinct ethnic group. Our analysis, controlling for seriousness and prior record, found that Hispanics did go to jail more often than whites, but, once again, the results were not statistically significant. First-time Hispanic offenders facing less than a year in jail were jailed 4 percent of the time compared to none of their white counterparts (phi = .14, n.s.); 30 percent of the first-time Hispanic offenders facing longer sentences were incarcerated compared to none of the comparable whites (phi = .42, p < .01: Although this particular finding is significant, it may be due, in part, to the small sample size [n = 39]); 42 percent of Hispanic repeat offenders facing less serious charges were sent to jail compared to 32 percent of their white counterparts (phi = .11, n.s.); and 72 percent of Hispanic repeat-offenders facing serious charges were incarcerated compared to 61 percent of similar whites (phi = .12, n.s.).

15. We compared the hearing lengths for offenders who spoke English proficiently and those who were not fluent in English. The hearings were, on average, the same length (between 1 and 2 minutes for both groups). Unfortunately, not all the observers noted which of the non-English speaking defendants caused problems because of their language needs, which prevented us from statistically determining the accuracy of this observation.

16. Repeat offenders charged with serious offenses were incarcerated 59 percent of the time if they spoke English compared with 82 percent of those who did not (phi = .22, p < .01). Similarly, English speaking repeat offenders charged with less serious offenses were jailed 33 percent of the time compared with 49 percent of their counterparts who did not speak English (phi = .14, p < .05).

17. We had also wanted to compare appointed and elected judges. Judges who are elected may be more likely than appointed justices to represent the concerns of their constituents. Appointments are made by the governor, and, such justices may better represent the criminal justice opinion of the state's chief executive, his staff, or American Bar Association committees (who often provide lists of candidates for judicial openings). Judges' elections or appointments may impact their sentencing decisions. Most of the judges (n = 10) whom we observed were appointed; two were elected. On the one hand, one of the elected judge's incarceration rate (the percentage of individuals he sent to jail) was 18.4 percent, which placed him toward the lenient end of the judicial sentencing spectrum. On the other hand, the second elected judge was one of our outliers (discussed later in this chapter), sentencing more than 90 percent of defendants to jail. Any analysis based on comparisons of these two judges with their colleagues, we felt, would be of little value.

18. White judges incarcerated 60 percent of those whose possible maximum sentences were at least one year, while nonwhite judges jailed only 40 percent of the offenders in this category (phi = .16, p < .01). White judges sentenced to jail 20% of offenders whose possible maximum sentence was less than one year, and nonwhite judges incarcerated 12 percent of the same group (phi = .07, p < .05). White judges sentenced to jail two-thirds of those offenders with prior records who faced severe penalties; the nonwhite judges incarcerated one half of the same group (phi = .12, p = .10).

19. We did not exclude any lenient judges because none were statistically different from the norm in their sentencing decisions.

20. Sixteen percent of white offenders who faced less than one year in jail were incarcerated by white judges compared to 24 percent of their nonwhite counterparts (phi = .10, p < .01) and 53 percent of whites who faced more than one year in jail were sent to jail by white judges compared to 68 percent of similar offenders who were minority members (phi = .16, p < .01).

21. Offenders who faced one year or more in jail on their charges were significantly more likely to be incarcerated by female judges; male judges incarcerated 47 percent of such offenders contrasted with the 63 percent jailed by female judges (phi = .16, p < .01). Judicial gender did not significantly influence sentencing decisions for repeat offenders facing less serious charges; 33 percent of repeat offenders facing incarceration for less than a year were jailed by male judges compared with 43 percent of their counterparts incarcerated by female judges (phi = .10, n.s.).

22. Two were private attorneys, one was a public defender, and one was county counsel.

23. Deterrence-oriented judges jailed 12 percent of those who they sentenced; rehabilitation-oriented justices incarcerated 16 percent; and incapacitation-oriented judges jailed 17 percent of these offenders.

24. Judges who told us they preferred the retribution philosophy sentenced to jail 48 percent of the repeat offenders who faced a possible maximum sentence of less than one year, compared to the other judges who incarcerated about one-third of similar offenders (phi = .17, p < .05).

25. It is not surprising that one of our outliers was a retribution-oriented judge.

26. Because of small cell sizes, we could not explore the differences for blacks or Asians, nor could we examine sentencing differences by gender for the same reason.

27. Length of hearing was not recorded for 107 cases, most often because the observers were uncertain about when the hearing began or concluded. Fifteen percent of the hearings lasted less than one minute (n = 222); 49 percent lasted one minute (n = 725); 23 percent lasted two minutes (n = 342); 8 percent lasted three minutes (n = 114) and 6 percent lasted four minutes or longer (n = 90). The longest timed hearing was fifteen minutes.

28. Twenty-seven percent of those with short hearings (one minute or less, n = 947) were incarcerated compared to 29 percent of those with intermediate hearings (2 or 3 minutes, n = 465) and 51 percent of those with lengthy hearings (4 or more minutes, n = 90).

29. Although the findings were significant for first-time offenders facing less than a year in jail, statistics were based on only three

incarcerated offenders (phi = .20, p < .05). The findings were not significant for first-time offenders facing a year or more in jail.

30. Half (51%) of those represented by attorneys were jailed compared with only 29 percent of those who appeared alone (phi = .12, p < .0001). When offense severity was considered, there were no differences between defendants appearing with or without counsel if they faced one year or more in jail. For defendants who faced incarceration for less than a year, however, 42 percent with counsel were incarcerated compared with only 18 percent of their counterparts without attorneys (phi = .12, p < .001).

31. Thirteen percent of those who could be jailed for one year or more had attorneys compared to only 4 percent of those who faced less time (phi = .15, p < .0001); 10 percent of repeat offenders had attorneys compared to only 1 percent of those without prior convictions (phi = .16, p < .0001); 5 percent of repeat offenders facing less than one year in jail had defense counsel compared to none of their counterparts without records (phi = .14, p < .001); 17 percent of repeat offenders facing a year or more in jail had attorneys compared to only 4 percent of first-time offenders confronting serious charges (phi = .15, p < .01).

32. Eight percent of defendants who were fluent in English had attorneys compared with only 3 percent of non-English speakers (Cramer's V = .09, p < .01) We did not consider offense severity nor prior record for this analysis due to too few cases (small cell sizes).

33. Although, if attorneys merely serve as a buffer between judges and defendants, translators could easily fulfill this purpose, eliminating or reducing non-English-speaking defendants' need for counsel.

34. These variables were: offense severity (33% of each sample faced serious charges); number of charges (about 61% of each sample faced one charge); prior record (67% of each sample had priors); appearance in custody (about 20% of each sample appeared in custody); offender ethnicity (48% of each sample were white); offender gender (about 84% of each sample were male); fluency in English (74% of each sample spoke English); judicial ethnicity (about 80% of each sample were sentenced by white judges); sentence philosophy (about 22% of each sample were sentenced by retribution-oriented judges); length of hearing (about 61% of each sample's hearings were one minute or less); presence of counsel (about 6% of each sample

were represented by counsel); and judicial status as an outlier (about 11% of each sample were sentenced by outlier judges).

35. We ran a separate logistic regression equation including only whites and Hispanics. The findings did not differ from the equations reported here.

36. Prejudicial career correlated highly with judicial ethnicity (correlation = .88), gender concordance was highly associated with judicial gender (correlation = .75), and ethnic concordance was highly correlated with defendant ethnicity (correlation = .85).

CHAPTER 6

1. The median fine for the current study was $150, with the range spanning $5 to $4,000 (only 4 fines exceeded $1,000).

2. Others have noted that lower court judges do not always possess a legal education (e.g., Ashman, 1975; Rottman, Flango & Lockley, 1995, pp. 70–76), however, all of the judges in our sample had law degrees. Certainly, this stems from legislated requirements that municipal court judges in California must be admitted to the state bar and have five years practice in law. Judges educated in the law probably share certain attitudes and characteristics due to their legal indoctrination. These judges may differ from lay judges in sentencing philosophies, attitudes toward individual offenders, and willingness to utilize certain sanctions.

3. Cross tabulations indicated that the female judges were more likely to incarcerate offenders, but the differences between the genders disappeared when we removed the two outliers (the justices who incarcerated more than 90% of offenders) from the analyses. The logistic regression revealed a more severe sentencing pattern by the male judges in our sample. This statistical technique has the advantage in that it examines the effect of each independent variable while controlling for the effects of the remaining items. But it does not include as many cases in the analyses as does cross tabulations since any missing information excludes the entire case.

4. Two extralegal factors that receive much attention in the literature, offender ethnicity and gender, did not impact the likelihood of jail for our offenders; nonwhites were not more likely than whites nor were males more likely than females to be incarcerated.

Findings regarding the lack of impact of ethnicity and gender on judges' sentencing probably are related to our ability to include controls not often found in studies that rely on official government data. In addition to a host of legal variables, we collected data on many extralegal factors (organizational variables and characteristics of both offenders and judges). Once all these variables had been statistically controlled in the analyses, neither ethnicity nor gender impacted sentence severity.

5. This finding was significant $(p < .0001)$ in the cross tabulation analysis, but was not statistically significant in the logistic regression analysis, probably due to the fact that missing data caused us to lose nearly half the cases.

6. Male judges sentenced males more leniently than female offenders and female judges treated females better than male offenders, even when offense severity and prior record were controlled. White judges were less likely to incarcerate whites. When offense severity and prior record were controlled, white repeat offenders who faced less than one year in jail were less likely than their nonwhite counterparts to be sent to jail by white judges.

7. The advantage of legal counsel may lay with our belief that justices grant preferential treatment to those who are similar to themselves. When offenders obtain representation, they also gain spokespersons from within the courtroom work group. Instead of communicating with offenders, judges are able to deal with the attorneys with whom they share many characteristics, including a work site and a legal education.

Defendants without attorneys may suffer because their dissimilarities from the justices play more of a part in the courtroom drama. Some justices, for example, told us that the attitudes of defendants—a matter that may well be culturally established—was a consideration in their sentencing decisions and that they assess offenders' attitudes through their courtroom behavior. Defendants with attorneys, however, leave it to their counsel to make impressions on the judges.

8. Because of multicollinearity, we were unable to include this issue in our multivariate analysis.

9. In the infamous Scottsboro case, eight black youths were convicted and sentenced by a jury to death for the rape of two white girls, although medical and other evidence were presented at trial

that indicated that the two females had not been raped (*Powell v. Alabama*, 1932). As a postscript, one of the victims later confessed that neither woman had been raped while the other victim, still holding to her original complaint, stated that she had been raped by only six of the youths.

REFERENCES

Alfini, J.J. (1981). Introductory essay: The misdemeanor courts. *Justice System Journal*, 66, 5–12.

Alfini, J.J. and Passuth, P.M. (1981). Case processing in state misdemeanor courts: The effect of defense attorney presence. *Justice System Journal*, 6, 100–116.

Andenaes, J. (1975). General prevention revisited: Research and policy implications. *Journal of Criminal Law and Criminology*, 66, 338–65.

Ares, C., Rankin, A., and Sturz, H. (1963). The Manhattan bail project: An interim report on the use of pretrial parole. *New York University Law Review*, 39, 67–92.

Ashman, A. (1975). *Courts of Limited Jurisdiction: A National Survey*. Chicago: American Judicature Society.

Bartollas, C., Miller, S.J., and Wice, P.B. (1983). *Participants in the Criminal Justice System: The Promise and the Performance*. Englewood Cliffs, NJ: Prentice Hall.

Beccaria, C. (1983). *An Essay on Crimes and Punishments*. Brookline Village, MA: Branden Press. (Translated and reprinted from *Dei delitti e delle pene*, 4th ed., 1775, London: F. Newberry.)

Beck, A.J., Bonczar, T.P., and Gilliard, D.K. (1993). *Jail Inmates 1992*. Washington, DC: Bureau of Justice Statistics.

Bedau, H. (1964). Death sentences in New Jersey 1907–1960. *Rutgers Law Review*, 19, 1–64.

Berger, M. (1976). Equal protection and criminal sentencing: Legal and policy considerations. *Northwestern University Law Review, 71,* 29–65.

Berkson, L. (1982). Women on the bench: A brief history. *Judicature, 65,* 286–93.

Black, D. (1980). *The Manners and Customs of the Police.* New York: Academic Press.

Blumberg, A.S. (1967). *Criminal Justice.* Chicago: Quadrangle Books.

Boland, B., Mahanna, P., and Sones, R. (1992). *The Prosecution of Felony Arrests, 1988.* Washington, DC: Government Printing Office.

Brickey, S.L. and Miller, D.E. (1975). Bureaucratic due process: An ethnography of a traffic court. *Social Problems, 22,* 688–97.

Bridges, G.S., Crutchfield, R.D., and Simpson, E.E. (1987). Crime, social structure and criminal punishment: White and nonwhite rates of imprisonment. *Social-Problems, 34,* 345–61.

Bullock, H. (1961). Significance of the race factor in the length of prison sentences. *Journal of Criminal Law, Criminology, and Police Science, 52,* 411–17.

California Judges Association. (1990). California Code of Judicial Conduct. In T.D. Morgan and R.D. Rotunda (eds.), *Model Code of Professional Responsibility, Model Rules of Professional Conduct, and Other Selected Standards, Including California Rules on Professional Responsibility.* Westbury, NY: Foundation Press. (Reprinted from California Code of Judicial Conduct, 1987, California Judges Association.)

Carbon, S., Houlden, P., and Berkson, L. (1982). Women on the state bench: Their characteristics and attitudes about judicial selection. *Judicature, 65,* 295–305.

Chiricos, T.G. and Bales, W.D. (1991). Unemployment and punishment: An empirical assessment. *Criminology, 29,* 701–24;

Chiricos, T.G. and Waldo, G.P. (1975). Socioeconomic status and criminal sentencing: An empirical assessment of a conflict proposition. *American Sociological Review, 40,* 753–72.

Cramer, J.A. (1981). Judicial supervision of the guilty plea hearing. In J.A. Cramer (ed.), *Courts and Judges*. Beverly Hills: Sage.

Daly, K. (1994). Gender and punishment disparity. In G.S. Bridges and M.A. Myers, *Inequality, Crime, and Social Control*. Boulder: Westview Press.

Davis, S. (1993). The voice of Sandra Day O'Connor. *Judicature*, 77, 134–39.

Davis, S., Haire, S., and Songer, D.R. (1993). Voting behavior and gender on the U.S. courts of appeals. *Judicature*, 77, 129–33.

Eisenstein, J. and Jacob, H. (1977). *Felony Justice: An Organizational Analysis of Criminal Courts*. Boston: Little, Brown.

Emmert, C. and Glick, H. (1987). Selection systems and judicial characteristics: The recruitment of state supreme court judges. *Judicature*, 70, 228–35.

Feeley, M.M. (1979). *The Process Is the Punishment: Handling Cases in a Lower Criminal Court*. New York: Russell Sage Foundation.

Flango, V.E. and Ducat, C. (1979). What differences does method of judicial selection make? Selection procedures in state courts of last resort. *Justice System Journal*, 5, 25–44.

Frankel, M. (1973). *Criminal Sentences: Law without Order*. New York: Hill and Wang.

Fukurai, H., Butler, E.W., and Krooth, P. (1993). *Race and the Jury: Racial Disenfranchisement and the Search for Justice*. New York: Plenum.

Garfinkel, H. (1949). Research note on inter- and intra-racial homicides. *Social Forces*, 27, 369–81.

Geis, G. (1979). Misdemeanors and the criminal justice system. *American Behavioral Scientist*, 22, 678–96.

Gilligan, C. (1982). *In a Different Voice: Psychological Theory and Women's Development*. Cambridge: Harvard University Press.

Glick, H. and Emmert, C. (1986). Stability and change: Characteristics of state supreme court judges. *Judicature*, 70, 107–112.

Goldman, S. (1985). Reaganizing the judiciary: The first term appointments. *Judicature, 68*, 313–29.

Gordon, M.A. and Glaser, D. (1991). The use and effects of financial penalties in municipal courts. *Criminology, 29*, 651–76;

Gottfredson, D.M. (1981). Sentencing guidelines. In H. Gross and A. von Hirsch (eds.), *Sentencing.* New York: Oxford University Press. (Adopted from L.T. Wilkins, J.M. Kress, D.M. Gottfredson, J.C. Calpin, and A.M. Gelman, *Sentencing Guidelines: Structuring Judicial Discretion*, 1978, Washington, DC: GPO.)

Green, E. (1961). *Judicial Attitudes in Sentencing: A Study of the Factors Underlying the Sentencing Practice of the Criminal Court of Philadelphia.* New York: St. Martin's Press.

Green, E. (1964). Inter- and intra-racial crime relative to sentencing. *Journal of Criminal Law, Criminology and Police Science, 55*, 348–58.

Hagan, J. (1974). Extra-legal attributes and criminal sentencing: An assessment of a sociological viewpoint. *Law and Society, 8*, 357–83.

Hagan, J. and Bumiller, K. (1983). Making sense of sentencing: A review and critique of sentencing research. In A. Blumstein et al., (eds.), *Research on Sentencing: The Search for Reform*, vol. II. Washington, DC: National Academy Press.

Holmes, M.D., Hosch, H.M., Daudistel, H.C., Perez, D.A., and Graves, J.B. (1993). Judges' ethnicity and minority sentencing: Evidence concerning Hispanics. *Social Science Quarterly, 74*, 496–506.

Hood, R. and Sparks, R. (1970). *Key Issues in Criminology.* New York: McGraw-Hill.

Inciardi, J.A. (1990). *Criminal Justice*, 3rd ed. New York: Harcourt Brace Jovanovich.

Jacob, H. (1980). *Crime and Justice in Urban America.* Englewood Cliffs, NJ: Prentice Hall.

Jesilow, P., Geis, G., Song, J.H.L., and Pontell, H. (1992). Culture conflict revisited: Fraud by Vietnamese physicians in the United States. *International Migration, 30*, 201–24.

Johnson, G.B. (1941). The Negro and crime. *Annals of The American Academy of Political and Social Science, 217,* 93–104.

Jones, D.A. (1981). *The Law of Criminal Procedure: An Analysis and Critique.* Boston: Little, Brown.

Judicial Council of California. (1992). *1992 Annual Report.* Vol. II: Judicial Statistics for Fiscal Year 1990–1991.

Kleck, G. (1981). Racial discrimination in criminal sentencing: A critical evaluation of the evidence with additional evidence on the death penalty. *American Sociological Review, 46,* 783–805.

Kleck, G. (1985). Life support for ailing hypotheses: Modes of summarizing the evidence for racial discrimination in sentencing. *Law and Human Behavior, 9,* 271–85.

Klein, A.R. (1988). *Alternative Sentencing: A Practitioner's Guide.* Cincinnati: Anderson Publishing.

Klein, S.P., Ebener, P., Abrahamse, A., and Fitzgerald, N. (1991). *Predicting Criminal Justice Outcomes: What Matters?* Santa Monica, CA: Rand Corporation.

Knowles, L.L. and Prewitt, K. (1969). *Institutional Racism in America.* Englewood Cliffs, NJ: Prentice-Hall.

Kunkle, W.J. (1989). Punishment and the criminal justice system: A prosecutor's viewpoint. In F.E. Baumann and K.M. Jensen (eds.), *Crime and Punishment: Issues in Criminal Justice.* Charlottesville: University Press of Virginia.

Lemert, E.M. and Rosberg, J. (1948). The administration of justice to minority groups in Los Angeles County. *University of California Publications in Culture and Society, 2,* 1–28.

Levin, M.A. (1977). *Urban Politics and Criminal Courts.* Chicago: University of Chicago Press.

Lindquist, J.H. (1988). *Misdemeanor Crime: Criminal Trivial Pursuit.* Newbury Park, CA: Sage.

Lipetz, M.J. (1980). Routine and deviations: The strength of the courtroom workgroup in a misdemeanor court. *International Journal of the Sociology of Law, 8,* 47–60.

Lizotte, A.J. (1978). Extra-legal factors in Chicago's criminal courts: Testing the conflict model of criminal justice. *Social Problems, 25*, 564–80.

MacNamara, D.E.J. (1977). The medical model in corrections: Requiescat in Pace. *Criminology, 14*, 439–47.

Mann, C.R. (1995). The contribution of institutionalized racism to minority crime. In D.F. Hawkins (ed.), *Ethnicity, Race and Crime: Perspectives Across Time and Place*. New York: SUNY Press.

Martin, E. (1990). Men and women on the bench: Vive la difference? *Judicature, 77*, 204–208.

Martin, E. (1993). The representative role of women judges. *Judicature, 77*, 166–73.

Martin, R. (1934). The defendant and criminal justice. *Bulletin No. 3437*. Bureau of Research in the Social Sciences, University of Texas.

McCall, G.J. (1978). *Observing the Law: Field Methods in the Study of Crime and the Criminal Justice System*. New York: The Free Press.

McClay, J.B. and Matthews, W.L., (eds.). (1991). *Corpus Juris Humorous: A compilation of Humorous, Extraordinary, Outrageous, Unusual, Colorful, Infamous, Clever, and Witty Reported Judicial Opinions and Related Materials Dating from 1256 A.D. to the Present*. Santa Ana, CA: Mac-Mat.

Meeker, J.W., Jesilow, P., and Aranda, J. (1992). Bias in sentencing: A preliminary analysis of community service sentences. *Behavioral Sciences and the Law, 10*, 197–206.

Meeker, J.W. and Pontell, H.N. (1985). Court caseloads, plea bargains, and criminal sanctions: The effects of Section 17 P.C. in California. *Criminology, 23*, 119–41.

Mileski, M. (1971). Courtroom encounters: An observation study of a lower criminal court. *Law and Society Review, 5*, 473–538.

Moran, T.K. and Cooper, J.L. (1983). *Discretion and the Criminal Justice Process*. Port Washington, NY: Associated Faculty Press.

Myers, M.A. (1987). Economic inequality and discrimination in sentencing. *Social Forces, 65*, 746–66.

Myers, M.A. and Talarico, S.M. (1988). *The Social Contexts of Criminal Sentencing.* New York: Springer/Verlag.

Nardulli, P.F. (1978). *The Courtroom Elite: An Organizational Perspective on Criminal Justice.* Cambridge, MA: Ballinger.

Neubauer, D.W. (1976). *Criminal Justice in Middle America.* Morristown, NJ: General Learning Press.

Neubauer, D.W. (1984). *America's Courts and the Criminal Justice System* (2nd ed.). Monterey, CA: Brooks/Cole.

Pepinsky, H.E. and Jesilow, P. (1984). *Myths that Cause Crime.* Washington, D.C.: Seven Locks Press.

Petersilia, J. and Turner, S. (1985). *Guideline-Based Justice: The Implications for Racial Minorities.* Santa Monica, CA: Rand Corporation.

Pommersheim, F. and Wise, S. (1989). Going to the penitentiary: A study of disparate sentencing in South Dakota. *Criminal Justice and Behavior, 16,* 155–65.

President's Commission on Law Enforcement and Administration of Justice. (1967). *Task Force Report: The Courts.* Washington, DC: Government Printing Office.

Ragona, A. and Ryan, J.P. (1983). Misdemeanor courts and the choice of sanctions: A comparative view. *Justice System Journal, 8,* 199–221.

Rottman, D.B., Flango, C.R., and Lockley, R.S. (1995). *State Court Organization.* Washington, DC: Bureau of Justice Statistics.

Ryan, J.P. (1980–81). Adjudication and sentencing in a misdemeanor court: The outcome is the punishment. *Law and Society Review, 15,* 79–108.

Sellin, T. (1928). The Negro criminal: A statistical note. *Annals of The American Academy of Political and Social Science, 140,* 52–64.

Selke, W.L. (1993). *Prisons in Crisis.* Bloomington, IN: Indiana Press.

Smith, R.L. (1987). The elephant in my living room. *Crime and Delinquency, 33,* 317–24.

Spohn, C. (1990). The sentencing decisions of black and white judges: Expected and unexpected similarities. *Law and Society Review*, 24, 1197–1216.

Steiner, J. and Brown, R. (1927). *The North Carolina Chain Gang*, Chapel Hill: University of North Carolina Press.

Stevenson, M.J. (1993, January 8). Muni court cuts its community service terms. *Los Angeles Daily Journal*, pp. 1, 12.

Uhlman, T.M. (1977). The impact of defendant race in trial-court sanctioning decisions. In J.A. Gardiner (ed.), *Public Law and Public Policy*. New York: Praeger.

Uhlman, T.M. (1979). *Racial Justice: Black Judges and Defendants in an Urban Trial Court*. MA: Lexington Books.

U.S. Bureau of the Census, Census of the Population 1970. (1973). *Subject Reports: Occupational Characteristics*. Washington, DC: Government Printing Office.

U.S. Bureau of the Census, Census of the Population 1990. (1992). *Supplementary Reports: Detailed Occupation and Other Characteristics from the EEO File for the United States*. Washington, DC: Government Printing Office.

Vines, K. (1962). The selection of judges in Louisiana. *Tulane Studies in Political Science*, 8, 99–119.

von Hirsch, A. (1981). Control of discretion: Guidelines and standards. In H. Gross and A. von Hirsch (eds.), *Sentencing*. New York: Oxford University Press.

Webber, D. and Nikos, K. (1992, November 16). Dwindling service sentences to cost millions in free labor. *Daily News*, pp. 1, 6.

Welch, S., Gruhl, J., and Spohn, C. (1984). Sentencing: The influence of alternative measures of prior record. *Criminology*, 22, 215–27.

Wice, P.B. (1985). *Chaos in the Courthouse: The Inner Workings of the Urban Criminal Courts*. New York: Praeger.

Zatz, M.S. (1984). Race, ethnicity, and determinate sentencing: A new dimension to an old controversy. *Criminology*, 22, 147–71.

Zatz, M.S. (1985). Pleas, priors, and prison: Racial/Ethnic differences in sentencing. *Social Science Research*, 14, 169–93.

Cases Cited

Bradwell v. Illinois 83 U.S. 130, 21 L.Ed. 442 (1872).

Brown v. Board of Education 347 U.S. 483, 74 S.Ct. 686, 98 L.Ed. 873 (1954).

Gong Lum v. Rice 275 U.S. 78 (1927).

In Re Jesus Ramirez Tuolumne County, Case No. 516 (1851).

McLaughlin v. Florida 379 U.S. 184, 85 S.Ct. 283, 133 L.Ed.2d 222 (1964).

Plessy v. Ferguson 163 U.S. 537, 16 S.Ct 1138, 41 L.Ed. 256 (1896).

Powell v. Alabama 287 U.S. 45, 5 S.Ct. 55, 77 L.Ed. 158 (1932).

Tate v. Short 401 U.S. 395, 91 S.Ct. 668, L.Ed.2d 130 (1971).

United States v. Gonzales United States District Court, New Mexico Territory Sessions (1881).

INDEX